MW00960746

Children I Have Loved, Lessons I Have Learned

---

a memoir

By

Pamela Stanfield

Copyright @ 2014 Pamela Stanfield

All rights reserved. No part of this book may be
reproduced, stored in a retrieval system, or transmitted,
in any form or by any means, electronic, mechanical,
photocopying, recording, or otherwise, without the
written permission of the copyright holder.

Printed in the United States of America

ISBN 978-1-49-974673-0

Children I Have Loved, Lessons I Have Learned

a memoir

Children I Have Loved,
Lessons I Have Learned

I began my career in education over forty years ago, have taught at various grade levels, and served as an elementary principal for seventeen years. During those years, I have loved the thousands of children I have had the privilege of serving. As is normal, some children have stayed in my consciousness more than others. Perhaps it was personality, or simply a factor of the time I spent individually with certain children because of discipline concerns or emotional issues. Most of the children I have written about are the ones who struggled. It is through these struggles and the difficult times that I learned to be a better teacher, better principal, and a better person.

There were hundreds of other children, happy, healthy children, who brightened my days as well, who taught me to savor the joys and innocence of childhood. I delight in hearing about their successes and take great joy in the unexpected meetings when someone asks, "Do you remember me?" Those children also enriched my life and made me grow.

This book is based on my memories of the many children who touched my life. In some cases, I had access to personal notes from years past which I reviewed for details. I have changed the names of all the children in order to protect their privacy and that of their families. Names of physicians, therapists and school personnel have also been changed. The important piece in this reflective writing is that I am sharing what has stayed with me through the years, the memories that have taught me to be a better educator and to be a better person.

I have also been a university professor teaching teachers, counselors, and principals. As I encouraged my adult students to be reflective practitioners, I too, saw the need to reflect on my years of practice and ponder the lessons I have learned from these children I have loved. I dedicate this book to those precious children.

Critical Lessons Learned from Children

Humility

Shantel Wilson
Edward Donovan
Jake Mahoney
Brian Williams
Daniece and Danielle Valle

Hope

Brett Limmerson
Charles Farmer
Timmy Noah
Terry Bruns
Paul Candela

Respect

Francis Bonnert
Marie Lakeshaw
Alex Tesson
Jim Martin
Susan Swann

Acceptance

> *Jaron Dalton*
> *Charlie Kelly*
> *Dan Crankson*
> *Robert Spursia*
> *Ricky Langley*

Perseverance

> *Susan McAdams*
> *David Larson*
> *David and Donald Turner*
> *Caroline Abernathy*
> *Wayne Hawkins*

Advocacy

> *Brian Mann*
> *Kaitlin Carson*
> *Billy Frampton*
> *DeWayne Puckett*
> *Clark Warner*

Humility

Shantel Wilson
Edward Donovan
Jake Mahoney
Brian Williams
Daniece and Danielle Valle

Shantel Wilson

Shantel was in that first class of third graders. I don't remember a great deal about her except that she wore her hair in braids, had skin the color of milk chocolate, and ate fried bologna for breakfast. She also was the bane of my existence. As I teach future teachers and principals now, I remind them that some of their best "professional growth opportunities" are sitting in the seats of their classrooms. Shantel was certainly a professional growth opportunity for me. She challenged me daily, questioning my instructions and directions. She wanted the classroom routines to suit her preferences. She talked incessantly. I struggled to accept her, to like her, to love her.

As a new teacher, I had the privilege of working with experienced teachers who were willing to listen to my frustrations and offer helpful ideas and suggestions. My principal was an older woman, quite the plump grandmotherly type, who was supportive and kind. Unfortunately, the school schedule did not allow much time for conversation among colleagues, so any discussions had to take place before or after the school day.

After one particularly trying day with Shantel, I was frustrated, almost angry about her behavior and the distraction she was causing in the class. On a personal level, I was annoyed that such a tiny child was able to challenge me as her teacher on such a regular basis and I seemed powerless to stop it. That night we had a regularly scheduled parent teacher meeting in the gym and all teachers were expected to attend. Parent turnout was not huge, but many parents were involved in the life of the school, so attendance was reasonable. I sat next to my third grade colleague and before the meeting started, I began to share my frustrations of the day, describing Shantel as a bratty little girl who just would not respond to my corrections. I was in full "let me tell you this" mode, when I felt a tap on my shoulder. I turned around to see who wanted my attention, and looked straight into the faces of Shantel and her mother. God did not honor my unspoken prayer to "take me now, Lord," and I was then faced with having to apologize profusely and try to undo some of the damage I had done.

Lessons Learned

Confidentiality, professionalism, and integrity are not simply words. They are critical needs in our profession.

We hold the lives of children in our hands and damaging words can inflict pain we can only imagine – even if done unintentionally.

Apologies are important, and are welcomed when sincerely given.

Forgiveness is precious.

Edward Donovan

I taught sixth grade in a suburban school district in the Midwest, and was somewhat experienced as a teacher, having taught for five years. In addition, I was married and had a child of my own, so had a better understanding of what parents expected and needed for their children.

That year I had a great group of students, most of whom were on grade level. The students were generally well behaved and got along fairly well so there were few discipline issues. There was one student who did not quite fit in with the group, however. Edward processed the concepts we were studying at a slower rate, and he had trouble paying attention. He was overweight and his appearance was sloppy. He would talk when he was supposed to be working and would disrupt the classroom. I worked with him one on one frequently to try to help him as he struggled with academics. I encouraged the other boys to include him in their recess games. His parents and I talked about his struggles and they willingly provided extra support at home. Nothing seemed to work and his behaviors continued to be disruptive. One habit in particular was for Edward to flop out of his chair onto the floor, somewhat like a beached whale. The other students would naturally laugh and the learning that was occurring would be interrupted.

After a few days of Edward's antics, I naturally was frustrated. I was upset with myself for not being able to focus Edward's energies in a more positive direction. As I stood at the chalkboard, writing a math problem, my back to the class, I heard a disturbance behind me, and without turning around, said in my most stern teacher voice, "Edward Donovan, get back into your seat, be quiet, and pay attention." Imagine my chagrin when I turned around and realized that Edward was not the culprit. Edward was not even in the room – he was absent. The students sat quietly looking at me, realizing at the same time, that I had unfairly singled out a student for correction. I apologized to them, and later that afternoon, called Edward, and apologized to him.

Lessons Learned

Don't jump to conclusions.

Don't correct a child publicly.

Apologies are opportunities for teaching.

Children can learn from our mistakes as well as their own.

Every child has value.

Jake Mahoney

Parent conferences were not top on my list as favorite ways to spend my time. As a fairly new teacher, I still was a bit intimidated by parents. I was well prepared for the conferences, but dreaded being questioned. I took it personally and felt as if the parents were questioning my ability to teach their children. During fall conferences with parents of my sixth grade students, I had prepared folders of student work and had all grades available for review should parents have questions about their child's performance. I remember thinking that I only had one more conference left that night – Jake Mahoney's. I was not anticipating any problems since Jake was a solid student who did fairly well in class. He was not a behavior problem.

Jake's mom came in and greeted me pleasantly. We looked at Jake's folder of work and his grades for the quarter. The grades were solid – B's and C's in his academic subjects, A's in art, music, and PE. At the end of the conference, Mrs. Mahoney looked at me and asked if I thought Jake was in the right reading group. (Those were the days when we placed students in the high, middle, and low reading groups.) Jake was in the middle group and seemed to be doing fairly well at that level. When I expressed my opinion and made a case for Jake in the middle group, his mother stated that she thought I was wrong, that Jake was not being challenged and should be in the high reading group.

I remember thinking "How dare you question me and what I think best for your child? I know the three groups and what takes place in each one." I did not express my thoughts to Mrs. Mahoney. In fact, I don't remember what I actually said, but I ultimately agreed to place Jake in the higher reading group. I confess the perverse part of my nature was at work here – somewhat of an "I'll show you" attitude. Jake began working with the higher reading group during the next quarter. And he excelled! Not only did he do well in Reading, but his academic performance in other curricular areas improved as well. He consistently made A's and B's for the remainder of the year.

At the time, I remember feeling ashamed of myself for the thoughts I had during and after the parent teacher conference. I learned a valuable lesson that day, and even though I probably never confessed to Mrs. Mahoney that she taught me a powerful lesson about being a teacher, I trust that she knew. What she doesn't know is how many times I have shared her story with beginning teachers so that they can learn from my mistakes.

Lessons Learned

We do not always "know what is best."

Parents are valuable partners in educating children.

When you learn not to be defensive in conversations and discussions, real problem solving can occur.

Brian Williams

I went to visit Brian last night. It was such a surreal experience - on the one hand, I was simply talking to Brian, a former student. On the other, I was talking to a man who had killed another human being. I am still struggling with how bizarre it seems.

Walking through the metal detector and handing my driver's license to the man behind the desk was a new experience for me. I was handed a plastic laminated card with a metal chain, which indicated the door I was to walk through, the floor I was to go to, and the booth I was to look for when the 8 pm visit for inmates was announced.

I sat in the waiting area, alone at first, but then surrounded by others when the visit time drew closer. Most of the visitors were women, some with small children. A few couples were present. I wondered if they were here to see their child. Most seemed very aware of the procedures and knew to place items in the small lockers provided. All we carried with us as we boarded the elevators were the plastic cards.

I arrived at booth four on the sixth floor, a partitioned area with a white plastic lawn chair. A phone was on the concrete wall that separated my booth from the one next to me. I could see the area inside through the plastic glass. The cubicle was the size of a phone booth and the door on the other side

11

was propped open by a plastic chair similar to the one I was sitting on. I could see into a larger space where two young men were seated at a table. They appeared to be playing a card game. I wondered if I would recognize Brian. I wondered what we could possibly talk about for forty minutes. I wondered if he were as nervous as I was.

When we first saw each other, we smiled tentative smiles. I recognized Brian and saw the little boy he once was when he was a student at the elementary school where I had been his principal. He looked different now – a young man of twenty with gold teeth, tattoos on his arm and his neck, and thick dreadlock hair. He was heavier - certainly not the small child from years ago. We began to talk about his family – his grandmother, his cousins and his aunts and uncles. He showed me a picture of his two year old son and showed me the tattoo on his neck – his name. The tattoo on his arm was the word ROCK – said kids had called him that for years and when he was fourteen, another kid wrote that on his arm, tattooing it with an ink pen. Later he had it re done as a real tattoo.

We talked about how he spent his time, with his day starting at 7am for breakfast. He has a single cell because he signed up for one shortly after he arrived. He prefers to be alone and does not want to share a cell. He described the layout of the jail – eight floors, four pods to a floor, with forty-eight cells to a pod. When I asked if it was scary, he said no, it was like being in high school and living in a dorm. He then told me this was his third time at this jail and he had only been in trouble once when someone punched him for no reason. He then got into a fight.

We talked about his earning a GED since he had been in jail. He was proud of that. I told him I was impressed by his writing when I read his letters and I encouraged him to write a journal, or at least letters to his son. We talked about reading and he told me he daydreamed so much, it was hard to focus on reading, but that now he had a lot of time, so maybe he would read more. He is looking forward to getting the book about card games that I told him about. He plays solitaire a lot and the book has twenty-one different ways to play. Since I can't mail the book to him, I will copy the pages and send with a letter.

We also talked about his legal situation. He said that when he arrived, he received letters from men in the penitentiary. I asked him how they knew him and he said they had seen his situation on the news and sent letters to offer him support. He told me he had a public defender but wasn't real happy with him – said he seemed scared when he talked to the prosecutor and the judge. He also said he thought all he could do was keep him from getting the death penalty. He mentioned that a lawyer wants to represent him for free and when I asked him why, he said his was a high profile case, said the lawyer had even sent him a text message before he turned himself in, saying to contact him and he would help

Brian turn himself in. I asked if he had been really scared when he was hiding and he said not really except when people started telling his family they would kill him when they found him. When he turned himself in, all the police were wearing protective vests and there were a lot of them.

One of the last things he said was "I think I can beat this." I did not respond.

Lessons Learned

When we teach students, we have no idea what the future holds for them.

No matter what the circumstances, we still feel connections to students we worked with and cared for.

Understanding the unthinkable may not be possible.

Sometimes we must respond to our hearts and not to our intellect.

Daniece and Danielle Valle

The discipline referral arrived in the office along with the Valle sisters. A huge hank of hair was taped to the referral with a note: " Daniece snatched this from Danielle's head when they were fighting."

Daniece was eleven years old and large for her age. She was tall and heavy set, and was one angry girl. The object of her anger was her sister Danielle. Danielle was the older sister, but had been retained, so both girls were in the fifth grade at our school. I do not remember the reason for the fight, but I do remember that even with placing the girls in separate areas of the office, the verbal fighting and insults continued. Each girl worked to make her comments more hurtful than the ones that had just been screamed across the room. The counselor and I each took a sister and attempted to calm them.

This screaming match and hair snatching was not the first incident. The girls consistently got into arguments with each other and with other girls who lived in their apartment complex. Anger seemed to surround them, and yet, there was often no discernible reason for the level of anger that was seen. We had tried all the traditional interventions – counseling, behavior plans, loss of privileges, rewards for good choices, letters and phone calls to parents. Nothing seemed to work.

I decided that a home visit was the strategy for today's incident, so I placed both girls in my car and drove less than two miles to the apartment complex where they lived. Since the phone had been disconnected, I had been unable to call home first to let the parents know I was coming and was bringing Daniece and Danielle home for the rest of the day.

When I arrived, both parents were at home. I was greeted with suspicion and even though words were not spoken, the perceived message was "Just who are you and what are you doing with our daughters?" We had talked on the phone in the past but had never formally met each other, so I explained who I was and why I had brought the girls home. The girls' demeanor at home was drastically different from what we had seen at school. They were very quiet, with heads down, and eyes cast to the floor. I began to describe the incident and was glad I had brought the discipline referral so that both parents could see physical evidence of the fight between the sisters.

It was obvious that the parents were angry. I was not sure whether they were angry with me or with their daughters for misbehaving. In an effort to connect with the parents and the frustration they were feeling, I remember stating "I understand how you must feel." That was when the father jumped to his feet, knocking a table over as he moved, and then screamed at me: "you don't understand, you can't begin to understand, when you look in the

17

mirror every morning, you see white skin. You are not black like me and you can never understand!"

I realized at that moment that I had walked into the home of a family, about whom I knew very little, that I had presumed they would be interested in talking with me because I was the principal at the school their children attended. I assumed that bringing the girls home was the best way to get parental support for better behavior at school. My naïve assumptions and my ignorance of the situation could have resulted in disaster.

I am not sure where the words came from. I was shocked by the vehemence with which the father spoke, but I simply said, "you are correct, I don't understand. I am not black, but I care about your daughters and am trying to understand. Please help me."

I wish I could say that the home visit that day was the beginning of a close relationship with the family and an improvement in the girls' behavior at school. Unfortunately, that was not the case. I do not remember the end of the conversation or what was said when I left that day, but I do remember that I was scared, sad, frightened, and much more aware of racial differences and tensions.

Lessons Learned

Never assume.

Never presume to know how someone else will respond.

Race matters.

You don't always know what is best for others.

Hope

Brett Limmerson
Charles Farmer
Timmy Noah
Terry Bruns
Paul Candela

Brett Limmerson

My skirt was hiked above my knees as I attempted to calm Brett while he was throwing a major temper tantrum on the floor of my office. I was on my knees trying to keep him from hitting himself. In desperation, I rubbed his back in a circular motion and sang a lullaby. My secretary asked how she could help and I asked her to contact the person in charge of special education in our district and request that she come immediately so she could see for herself what Brett was like. The counselor joined me and the two of us were barely able to contain Brett. He was thrashing and yelling, screaming at the top of his lungs. No one knew what had upset him.

Brett was new to our school that year and obviously had some emotional problems. His parents had good intentions, but because of their own histories, had very little knowledge about parenting. The father had grown up in an orphanage and the mother's parents had died when she was young, so she had been raised by grandparents. Brett was adopted and little was known about his medical history. Because neither parent had spent much time around small children, they were unaware that Brett's behavior was abnormal. There were days when Brett functioned in the classroom in a relatively normal fashion. He was bright and did well academically when he was focused on his work. More times than not, he would fly into a rage, with no seeming provocation.

The normal progression from a regular classroom to receiving special education services is a slow, carefully documented process. Because of the violent nature of Brett's episodes and the seeming lack of a trigger, the process was accelerated. Brett was placed directly into a day treatment program where he received academic instruction, counseling, and therapeutic care. The parents were also actively involved in counseling and family therapy to provide them with support as they struggled to help their son.

Brett was a child who remained on my heart, long after he left our school. We never did learn why he acted as he did, and I often wondered what the future held for him. How could a child that young be so emotionally disturbed? Would he ever get better? The prospects seemed dim.

Years later, I talked with the special education coordinator who had come to my office that first day, and I asked her about children we had both worked with. When we came to Brett, she broke into a huge smile and told me that he was one of the success stories. After years at the therapeutic placement, he was able to transition back to the regular public school and had graduated with his high school class. We both shed tears that day.

Lessons Learned

Family is important.

There is ALWAYS hope.

Children are resilient.

Charles Farmer

As a brand new teacher in an inner city school in Atlanta, Georgia, I was excited to begin my teaching career with the precious third graders who had been assigned to me. The class was a mix of races and abilities, which I expected. The child in my class with cystic fibrosis was not something I was prepared for. I knew nothing about the disease, and in my beginner's naiveté, I simply did not understand the impact that the disease would have upon me or the students in my class. I remember being compassionate and concerned when Charles' medical history was shared with me, but without any knowledge of the disease, his medical needs were an abstraction. I was more focused on beginning the year with well organized lessons and carefully prepared activities for my students. The first week of school, I began to get to know my students and started the first year of many where I would indeed love the children in my care.

At that point in time, teachers had no official planning time. We ate lunch with our students, took them to the park across the street to play after we ate, and spent the entire day with our students. At times, a music teacher would come to the class for a short period of time and I was able to leave the classroom, but that was not a regularly scheduled occurrence.

The first time Charles threw up at lunch, I was shocked. I remembered hearing about the thick mucus that clogged his lungs, but now the disease was reality, not a discussion of the abstract. As a young teacher, without children of my own, I had not been faced with cleaning up bodily fluids, and remember being frozen momentarily, before realizing it was up to me to handle the situation, to care for Charles, and to model for the rest of the children how we should react to an unpleasant situation. This was before the time of universal precautions and latex gloves, so I simply used paper towels to clean up the table and Charles. I then got him a new lunch tray, gave him a hug, sat next to him, and finished my own lunch. I confess to inwardly gagging as I ate the rest of my lunch, but knew the children were watching me. Charles vomited almost daily at lunch, but we as a classroom family came to a routine, where whoever was seated closest to Charles simply did the cleaning up, without much of a discussion. The third grade children surrounded Charles with an acceptance and love that has remained with me through the years.

Lessons Learned

Expect the unexpected, even when you have no knowledge of what that might be.

Teaching is filled with circumstances you never dreamed would affect you.

Remember always that your children are watching you – your every facial expression, your chosen words, your reactions.

The love of children for each other is a beautiful thing – something we adults can learn from them.

Timmy Noah

It was a standoff. Timmy was standing in the clinic, denying that he had pooped in his pants, while the nurse held the evidence in a plastic bag. Timmy insisted his older sister had messed in the pants and he simply put them on to wear to school that day. Timmy was probably one of the most stubborn children I ever met. He refused to accept his part in any situation. His defiance, even as a seven year old, was similar to what you might see with a street hardened teen. Timmy's mother was a single mom who wanted her children to do well in school. She was willing to help in any way.

There were days that Timmy would not comply with the simplest of requests, would defy his teacher, and would refuse to cooperate with any of the personnel in the building. A plan was developed which stated that Timmy would be given a set number of opportunities to do what was expected or consequences would follow. The consequences ranged from losing privileges to being taken home as a last resort. The first time I had to take Timmy home, it took two adults in the back seat of my car, one on each side, to keep Timmy from getting out of the car. He kicked the seats, the windows, the aide and the counselor, screaming the whole time. His mother was at home, and was wonderful with him. She was firm with him, and yet loving. She reinforced what he was hearing at school, so that he got a consistent message about what was expected. Her analysis of his behavior was that he was the baby of the family and that his older siblings and she had "spoiled him rotten."

Gradually over time, the trips home became fewer and fewer. The times we did have to take him home, he was able to sit in the backseat alone, even though he was angry. One trip home was memorable. Timmy was in the back, belted in, and we arrived at his house. Mom's phone had been cut off, so I was not sure she was home. I told Timmy to stay in the car while I went to the door. No answer. I returned to the car to find Timmy standing outside the car with one of the back doors open. He mumbled something. I finally figured out that he was telling me the door would not close. I tried it – he was right. There was a tiny latch that had been tripped keeping the door from closing. I walked to the other side, looked at what the latch was supposed to be, came back and tried to trip the latch. No luck. Back to the other door. I tried that latch, and before I knew it, I had a second door that would not close. This was out in the middle of nowhere before the days of cell phones.

I placed Timmy in the front seat, strapped the seatbelt across him and had him reach behind the seat to hold the back car door closed. I did the same on my side as I tried to drive back to school. If you have never driven with two open back doors, you may not realize that when you turn a corner or go around a curve, the door swings open. We slowly made our way back to town where I stopped at the first gas station I saw. The man who owned the station saw us coming and quickly came to our rescue with a quick twist of a screwdriver which tripped the latches back into place. When I asked him what I owed him, his answer was "not a thing, ma'am, not a thing!" I am sure he has told this story as many times as I have.

Timmy and I continued our drive back to school. I was quiet and stony faced, angry about the car fiasco. Timmy began to giggle, looking sideways at me. I couldn't help it. It was funny! By the time we returned, we were both laughing – not exactly the typical response when a child has been sent to the office for his defiant behavior. The secretary simply stared at us both as we made our way into my office where Timmy spent the remainder of the day. Timmy and I bonded that day. We shared an experience that no one else could possibly have understood. Timmy's behavior improved after that episode.

To this day, his photo, taken when he was a fourth grader, sits in my office with the question "What is best for the child?" written on the caption under the picture.

Timmy would be a young man in his thirties now. I often wonder where he is, what he is doing, and if he has any idea what a powerful impact he had upon my life.

Lessons Learned

Humor is a powerful equalizer.

Humor is a necessity.

Children can be our most influential teachers.

Serendipitous happenings can be turning points.

Terry Bruns

T erry met his father for the first time when he was ten years old, playing on a junior football team. He was on the sidelines waiting for the game to start when a man walked up to him and said "Are you Terry Bruns? Well, I'm your dad." Terry shared that story with me during one of the conversations we had when he was in the seventh grade. I was Terry's mentor, but we had known each other since he was in kindergarten and I was his principal.

Terry had been raised by his grandparents along with his two brothers. His mother lived out of state with two additional children. The grandparents were hard working people who wanted their children to grow up, work hard, and do well. Unfortunately, their daughter, Terry's mother, had given birth to five children with different men and had not followed the path her parents had dreamed for her. And now here they were trying to raise three grandsons, two of whom had difficulties. Terry had a big problem with anger and was consistently getting into fights at school. One of his younger brothers had some developmental delays and struggled with the most basic learning. He also had some unnatural fears which would cause him problems at times. He was deathly afraid of bugs and would refuse to go outside if he saw any insects at all.

I worked with the family throughout Terry's elementary school years and made numerous phone calls and home visits. There were times when his grandmother accused me of being a racist, picking on Terry for the stuff he did. His grandfather was more objective and realized that Terry would "act the fool" and needed to be disciplined.

When I retired, I owed the district a number of hours of volunteer service as part of an early retirement incentive plan. Rather than complete a project or work on curriculum, I decided I would rather mentor a student, so I called Terry to see what he thought about my joining him at the middle school one day a week beginning in the fall. There was dead silence on the other end of the phone, so I told him to talk about it with his grandparents and I would call back. When I reached his grandfather later that night, he laughed, saying Terry had not said a word to him. He said "that boy thought he was through with you Dr. Stanfield!" Grandpa thought the mentoring idea a good one so gave his permission for me to meet with Terry once a week at school to help him with his academics and his behavior.

Terry and I met once a week at the middle school for a year and a half. I attended his football games and watched him perform in a school play. I delivered Christmas presents to his home for him and his brothers. We had a good relationship and even his grandmother came to see that I truly cared about Terry and just wanted to help him.

In the middle of Terry's seventh grade year, his mom came back to town and Terry began to see more of her. I was able to meet her at one of the football games. While she was cordial with me, she was an angry woman who had been to the school upset about consequences Terry had received for fighting. She and Terry's grandmother had become so unruly that the building was placed on lockdown as soon as they left to go complain to the superintendent. I could see similarities in Terry's anger and that of his mother.

His mother and Terry's natural father got back together and asked Terry to come to live with them. I was worried because that meant Terry would be attending a middle school in another part of the city, not known for good schools. But I realized how important it was for Terry to spend time with his parents. He consistently acknowledged and praised his grandparents for taking him in and raising him, and appeared to have a real understanding of what a sacrifice that was for them, and yet he desperately wanted to have a dad and his own mom in his life, like the other kids did.

Terry has since been in two different schools. The last time I spoke to him, he said he was playing football but probably would not be able to play varsity ball next year unless he started doing better with his grades and staying out of trouble.

His grandparents send me a Christmas card every year.

Lessons Learned

Some kids have a special place in your heart.

Potential and possibility mean nothing without support.

Family ties can make a difference.

No matter how frustrating the circumstances, don't give up.

Paul Candela

I don't think I had ever heard a child cry as loudly as Paul. He did not cry like most children - he wailed, and he wailed so loudly that the walls of my office seemed to vibrate. The strange thing about Paul was that he really was not a difficult child, he just had a tendency to say or do the wrong thing and when corrected by an adult, he simply could not handle being held accountable for his actions. His only response was to wail.

Paul continued his wailing even when in fourth and fifth grades, long past the time most boys would dare to show tears. I liked Paul and worked long and hard to reach him, to teach him other ways of handling his frustration and anger. His teachers and the school counselor also spent time with him, but to no avail. When Paul left our school to go to middle school, we sent word that he would need some special attention from the counselor and principal if he were to succeed at that level.

Paul came from a poor home and rode the bus for an hour to get to school. His mother wanted him to get the best education possible so she signed him up for the city county transfer program which meant that Paul attended school far away from his neighborhood and his friends. He wasn't the strongest student academically, but he had a mom who supported and pushed him, who held high expectations for him.

It is interesting that I don't remember the details about Paul's referrals to the office. What I remember is that tear stained face and the reverberating wails that still hurt my ears. No matter how often he would promise that he would talk through whatever the problem was in the future, he would lapse into the only response he knew, which was to wail. On days when he did not get into trouble, Paul's smile could brighten anyone's day – such a contrast.

I often thought about Paul as he moved on to the middle school and then the high school, wondering if he was still the wailer that held the crying record for my office. Imagine my surprise when Paul visited me one day after school. Now a young man almost six feet tall, with a deep voice, and the bristles of a beard, Paul gave me a bear hug and said he just had to come back to see his elementary school and his "old" principal. He asked me if I remembered him and how he used to cry when he came to my office. I assured him he still held the record! Paul was a senior in high school, planning to graduate in a few months. He was going to go to college and would be the first in his family to do so. And he told me that if not for his mother who had supported him every single day, or the teachers who had made him study and expected him to behave, and me as his principal who had spent so much time with him, accepting him for who he was, that he would probably be on the streets like some of his old neighborhood friends.

Paul hugged me again before he left and told me I was going to be proud of him someday. I told him I already was.

Lessons Learned

A mother's love is a powerful motivator.

Sometimes just being there is enough.

A kid can beat the odds.

Respect

Francis Bonnert
Marie Lakeshaw
Alex Tesson
Jim Martin
Susan Swann

Francis Bonnert

Crossed eyes. Buck teeth. Coarse woolly hair. Tall and gangly. Too big for his nine year old body. Limited verbal skills. A sad but sweet child who did not know what to do when someone made him angry.

Francis taught me about "yo mama." Even though I had taught African American children during my nine years in the classroom, I had not experienced the angry response that "yo mama" evoked in young black males. My first year as a principal, Francis made frequent trips to my office because he was so easily angered and would scream, yell, and cry. The first time I tried to figure out what had happened, all he would say was something about his mother. I asked if something was wrong with her. I was on a totally different conversational level, and totally oblivious to the fact that I was ignorant of his culture. Since Francis had limited verbal skills, it took quite awhile, but I finally discerned that the words "yo mama" were fighting words and he was defending his mother's honor. I kept trying to get him to look at me as he talked but he kept his eyes downcast. I learned then that in his home if he were in trouble, he had better be looking at the floor. What a confusing world for this child – at home he was taught one thing, and at school, we were asking something very different. Francis was patient with me, giving me tiny glimpses into his culture and world, which helped me as his principal begin to help him.

One day I remember with extreme clarity. Francis had been sent to the office once again for his out of control anger. He was in the outer office thrashing about, screaming, and I had just approached him to bring him into my office when my superintendent arrived unannounced. There I was squatting in front of this angry child while the superintendent watched his brand new principal handle the situation. I remember leaning close to Francis and whispering in his ear, telling him I really needed his help, that my boss was there and I needed to talk with Dr. Triffith, but would be there to help him just as soon as I could. Miraculously, Francis stopped his screaming and began to settle. The superintendent thankfully did not stay long, but he did turn as he left and said "By the way, if you need to hear this, you are doing a good job. Keep it up."

I am forever in Francis' debt – not just for making me look good in front of my superintendent, but for teaching me about young black males and how to build relationships across cultural and gender differences one small step at a time. The last time I saw Francis, he was in his teens and was in a children's home I was touring as part of a conference. I never got the details as to why he was there, so could only imagine. He recognized me and we shared an emotional hug that day.

Lessons Learned

Sometimes we don't know what we don't know.

We can learn from those who are different from us.

Learning comes in unexpected ways, from the most unlikely sources.

Marie Lakeshaw

"It is a very rare medical disorder. She is non verbal and we really don't know what her cognitive abilities are. She is in a wheelchair and needs assistance with eating and drinking. She wears diapers. We think she can hear but are not sure if she has some hearing loss. She wears glasses. She drools. Her parents want her in a regular kindergarten classroom and want her to be treated like any other kindergarten child. They want her at your school."

... a message on my voice mail

Her future kindergarten teacher, Caroline, and I went to the pre-school where Marie was attending school to observe her and see just how we could manage her needs in a typical kindergarten classroom. There was a lot of assistance provided for almost every activity, including a great deal of physical involvement, lifting and positioning Marie so she could be on the floor with her peers, propped up in a special chair. We left the pre-school and began the drive back to our school. We didn't talk at first, both of us caught up in our own reactions and thoughts. Then the questions came, flooding the car with intensity. How could she function in a regular classroom? Why would her parents want her in that type of setting where she would not get nearly the individual attention she needed? What would the other parents think? How would the other children react to Marie? Would her needs keep the teacher from doing the job she expected from herself each year as she worked with twenty-five kindergarteners?

Caroline was an experienced teacher who was willing to take on the challenge, but was understandably nervous and concerned about the help she would need and how she could manage everything. As the building principal, I knew that Marie had every right to attend school in a regular setting – and was an advocate for inclusion, but I confess, after seeing Marie, I wondered if indeed this was truly what was best for her, and for all the other children. I called a friend and colleague with a background in special education, described Marie, and said "Talk to me! Help me remember why this is a good thing."

That first year was a challenge for all of us as we addressed all the potential problems and concerns. We held a parent meeting for the parents of children assigned to Caroline's class so they could meet Marie's parents and not be surprised on the first day of school when a child with such significant disabilities was in the same class with their children. We had arranged for a full time teacher assistant to be in the classroom to provide an extra set of hands. In addition, there were numerous special education teachers who provided various parts of Marie's instruction and physical therapy.

The other children loved Marie and we had to be careful that they didn't hover and treat her like a doll. They included her in their activities and play, grimacing when she drooled, which was an effective deterrent, much more so than anything the adults had tried. At the end of the year, I wondered if I would have any parent request for their child not to be in the same class with Marie in first grade. In fact, the opposite occurred. Parents saw what a positive effect Marie had on the other children and parents of children in other classes requested their children be in the same class as Marie.

Marie was with us throughout her elementary career. There were difficult periods as each year adjustments had to take place with new teachers and new students. In third grade, Marie bit her assistant, so was sent to the office with a discipline referral. I remember being in a bit of a quandary, unsure if Marie could comprehend anything I said. I decided to treat her as I would any child and spoke to her in a firm voice letting her know that biting was unacceptable. I then directed her to wheel her chair to my desk when she was sorry and was ready to return to class. Never really expecting that to happen, I was stunned when Marie wheeled her chair toward me. To this day, I really don't know how much Marie understood about the world around her, but I do know she learned to wheel her own chair, to take a drink from the water fountain, and to make her likes and dislikes known.

Marie moved to a different city a few years later and I would think about her, especially when I would see a cute little blonde girl, or when a colleague would reminisce about the times Marie would cry until she had to be removed from the classroom.

Marie died at the tender age of seventeen, simply going to sleep one night and not waking up. I attended a memorial service for her and shed tears as we watched the video showing the experiences she had shared at school and at home with her loving parents and sisters. She will always have a special place in my heart.

Lessons Learned

We do not always know what is best, even when we think we do.

Every single child has worth and value.

Every single child can learn.

Learning takes many different forms.

Most people are nice and accepting, willing to help.

A lifetime can be much shorter than we would ever dream it could be.

Alex Tesson

The huge chartered bus pulled into camp, the horn blaring to announce its arrival. Campers of all ages began to exit the bus and collect their luggage with the help of all the volunteers and counselors who were enthusiastically greeting each camper with whoops and yells. The procedure was to get each camper to the correct cabin, get all medications and specialized equipment to the nurse, and then off to the pool for the swimming test.

This week's camp was designed for children with serious illnesses, burns, and those with cancer. It was one week of the year when each kid could be normal, could swim, horseback ride, hike, canoe, fish, without having to worry about treatments and doctor visits. For many of the families, this was a much needed respite for the parents who spent untold hours dealing with serious medical issues that affected not just the child who was ill, but the entire family.

I was an adult volunteer who was chaperoning a group of high school students in our church youth group. I was expected to help out wherever needed, so worked in the office, did laundry, helped in the kitchen, and provided encouragement and support for the young adults from our church. I had lots of opportunities to interact with the campers as well. We had spent hours the night before the campers arrived learning their particular medical histories and needs. Each of our church volunteers was paired with a camper and helped to supervise a cabin of eight to ten campers ranging in ages from six to sixteen.

For whatever the reason, Alex and I connected. Alex was a twelve year old boy from Texas who had lost part of his leg to bone cancer. He was "all boy" with an energy and a bravado that electrified the air when you were around him. I remember him bounding off the bus that first day and being greeted as the "champ of camp." He had painted a huge smiley face on the stump of his leg and he could make it move with his muscles. The younger kids loved it. He would use his crutches or prosthesis to walk and run. I would see him each day at meals and then at the special event held each night. There were times I was in the clinic when he arrived to take his meds, and we would joke with each other.

Alex is the reason I completed the high ropes course at camp. His cabin group was scheduled to be at the course and he asked me to come watch him. I arrived with camera in hand, and watched in awe, as he removed his prosthesis, propped it against a tree, and climbed to the top of the first station. He moved from station to station on one leg, shouting and laughing the entire way, just thrilled to be so high in the air, doing what everyone else was able to do.

When he completed the course, he grabbed me and yelled that it was now my turn. I assured him that the course was just for the campers, but by then his entire cabin group was shouting for me to climb. I truly did not think I had the upper body strength to complete the course, but then Alex looked at me and said "if I can do it with one leg, surely you can do it with two."

I completed the high ropes course and Alex was there to greet me with a huge high five when I made it to the ground. That week was a special one for the two of us, and it was only the last day when one of my youth group said something that Alex learned I was a principal. That threw him completely – he could not believe that he actually had enjoyed spending time with someone from a school!

Alex and I spent four summers at camp. It was a meaningful experience for both of us and while we did write to each other during the winter months, we both looked forward to seeing each other at camp every summer. Alex's last summer at camp was bittersweet. His cancer had come back and he was on morphine for the pain the entire time he was at camp. I remember sitting under the stars with him, late one night, waiting for the line at the nurse's office to clear. I asked Alex if he ever was mad at God for the return of the cancer and his response was that "no, I know how to deal with this stuff – better me than some little kid." I knew that was his bravado speaking, and it was hard to hear. He had agreed to some experimental treatments but had decided he was tired of all that, so even though the words remained unspoken, both Alex and I knew that this summer would be his last summer at camp.

For Valentine's Day, the following February, my husband gave me an airline ticket to fly to Texas. I had never met Alex' family but his mother and I had spoken by phone many times. His family had just been evicted from their apartment the weekend I arrived, so I visited them as they were moving into another small apartment. His step dad seemed brusque, not sure what to make of this woman from another state who had come to see his step-son. His brother and sister knew me from camp and his mom and I connected the way moms do when they share a common bond.

Alex was in a hospital bed in the small living room. He recognized my voice and seemed to respond to the camp videos his family played while I was there. His stepdad continued moving furniture and boxes while I talked and sat with Alex. I can remember thinking at the time how very gracious they were to allow this perfect stranger to sit in their home with their child during what was certainly a tense and difficult time for them. Alex's mom showed me all the medications and equipment Alex needed. One entire section of the kitchen was filled with all the medical supplies. She had decided to go to school to become a nurse since she had learned so much through all of Alex' treatments and operations.

That night, Alex's stepdad bought us supper at a fast food restaurant and brought it home for us to eat. He and I then stood outside and looked at the dark sky filled with tiny stars. He spoke of his own youth growing up in the gangs, and finally breaking from that life to marry Alex's mother. He then said he loved Alex like he was his own son and that Alex had taught him more about life than any grown up. He then told me that the blue Mustang parked out front was for Alex because every sixteen year old boy needs a special first car.

Alex never got to drive the Mustang. He died two weeks after I visited. His name is engraved on a small brass plaque that has a permanent place on the wooden cross at summer camp. There is a new clinic at camp now and one of the rooms has a plaque hanging on the wall in memory of "the champ of camp."

Lessons Learned

A lot of living can happen in a short life.

Attitude counts.

Accept the challenges with grace and good humor.

You can learn about living from the dying.

Jim Martin

On a warm spring day, I walked into a neighboring school to attend a meeting for one of the students who attended school there. He was a first grader who had been diagnosed with significant behavioral issues, but who had made enough progress that he was being considered for placement in the regular school setting. He lived in our school's attendance area, so would be attending our school. The room was filled with many adults, including Jim's mother and grandmother. The room was also obviously filled with a great deal of tension. I did not know much about Jim or his needs so took my place at the table waiting for the meeting to begin.

After the initial introductions, the meeting began with a description of Jim's progress as well as his needs. The meeting had been in session only a few minutes before Jane, Jim's mother, exploded out of her chair, hitting the table with her fist, and screamed profanities and the question "What do I have to do to get my kid out of this school with all these lesbians?" Her mother tried to calm her down, touching her elbow gently and encouraging her to simply sit and listen to all that was being said. Jane was having none of that and continued to rant at all present. The chairman of the meeting ended the meeting, saying we would meet again at a later date. That meeting would be held in a district office and not at the school site. After Jane and her mother left, the school personnel shared with me that Jane was a very volatile and hostile parent who verbally harassed the teachers and administrators at the school. It had gotten so bad, she was not allowed in the school except to come directly to the office to pick up her son. The school staff had developed a plan where no one person was ever alone with Jane.

And all I could think is "this woman is coming to my school!" I was not as concerned about the child's behavioral issues as I was about his mother's. Our quiet suburban elementary school was not somewhere that parents screamed profanities and other slurs.

Jim did come to our school and his mother and I worked together throughout his years there. We began to work together when I invited Jane and her mother to meet with me before Jim ever came on the first day. We talked about what our school was like and how we wanted to help Jim be successful. Jane acknowledged that she had an anger management problem and was being treated with medication. She admitted that sometimes she did not take her medicine, so we agreed that if she had any concerns at all, she would come to me first and that if her anger was out of control, I could remind her to take her medicine before we would talk. We actually put our plan into writing and it served us well for most of the time when Jim was at our school.

We did have some serious incidents regarding Jim and other children. He antagonized one particular child who lived in the neighborhood who also attended our school. The other child's parents reported Jim to the police so a juvenile officer became involved with Jim early in his school career.

One day Jim came to school with lice and the school nurse had to send him home with the requisite instructions about removing nits. The next day Jim returned to school with his head completely shaved. He was humiliated and wanted to wear a hat to cover his bald head. Even though wearing hats was not allowed during the school day, we excused Jim and allowed him his hat.

Not long after that, he showed the nurse where he had been bitten by a dog on his head and where his mother had super glued the area back together. By this time, we were already working with social services to assist the family, so the case worker was called to intervene.

Jim was talented academically and was able to perform at a high level in his classes. However, he did not get homework done and appeared embarrassed by his home situation. I watched a cute little kid, with lots of energy and potential, withdraw into an unhappy and depressed boy, angry at the world.

I remember spending a late afternoon at an all district event where Jim got into an argument with another student. He was so angry, he was crying, which angered him even more. I was surprised when he agreed to walk away from the crowd and sit with me at the end of the football field. There he poured out his heart – about the father he did not know, his crazy mother who was always screaming at him and everyone else. The only person in his life that he felt like he could depend on was his grandmother and he knew she was elderly and not in good health. He was so incredibly sad, seeing no hope for his future. He wanted to know why other kids had moms and dads and got to play baseball and go to scouts. I had no answers for Jim. I simply sat and listened, hugging his shoulders, and wishing desperately that I did have some answers for him.

A few years later, I saw Jim when I visited the middle school he was attending. He assured me he was doing okay, but then told me his grandmother had died. There was such sadness on his face.

Lessons Learned

I learned I don't have all the answers.

Anger hurts.

Even when we try our hardest, we are not guaranteed happy endings.

Susan Swann

"As you know from our many conversations by phone and at the police station, Susan's behavior at the end of the day on Monday, October 25th has resulted in her being suspended from school......Because of her disrespect, defiance of authority, and violent behavior, Susan is being suspended from school for ten days.."

...excerpt from a letter to Susan's parents

When I was taking classes to become certified as a principal, if I had been told I would be responsible for the handcuffing of a fourth grade girl, I would have denied that such a thing could ever happen. Ten year olds are children. They are not hardened criminals!

Susan arrived at our school in her third grade year. She quickly made a name for herself by fighting with other students, and being extremely disrespectful and defiant when adults intervened to help resolve the problems. Ten office referrals that year brought her to the top of the concern list and school personnel worked with Susan and her parents to help her learn to handle her anger in a more appropriate way. Unfortunately, Susan's anger continued to be a concern with increasing referrals to the office in both fourth and fifth grade years. After a mental health evaluation, parents were strongly encouraged to seek professional help and counseling for Susan.

On one occasion, Susan was so angry that both her parents and I struggled simply to get her into the car for the ride home. Susan was screaming, kicking, biting, yelling, and threatening to hurt anyone close to her. She was angered about a bus incident earlier in the day when the bus driver reported that Susan kept hitting other children on the bus. Susan had an exceptionally difficult time taking responsibility for her actions and insisted that others were lying about her.

On the day Susan was arrested, she had become so violent that her safety and that of those around her was of great concern. The rest of the students in the classroom were asked to leave so that Susan was alone in the room with the counselor and the teacher. I was called to assist. By the time I arrived Susan was destroying the class and then ran from the room. We sent word for the secretary to call her parents and we tried to get Susan to the office where we could limit her access to the exits. We were afraid she would run in front of the cars and buses. Susan continued to be violent, screaming, and attacking the adults who were trying to help her. The police were called as a last resort, but since Susan's outbursts were more and more frequent, and parents had not followed through on strong encouragement to seek professional counseling, other options were non existent. The first officer attempted to direct Susan to be seated in a chair in the office, and before my eyes she changed from a fourth grade girl into a streetwise, cold, and hardened individual who cursed and refused to respond. She then raised her fist as if to hit the officer and the second officer then insisted she be cuffed and taken to the police station. I remember being stunned that a ten year old had to be handcuffed and yet also thankful that she was unable to hurt herself or anyone else. I cringed when the officers searched her pockets and she loudly proclaimed that "those are my crayons." A fourth grader. Handcuffs. The two do not go together.

Both the counselor and I followed the officers to the police station where we met with Susan's parents, and once again urged them to seek help for Susan and her uncontrollable rages. Naturally, they were upset and angry that their child was involved with the police. Our hope was that perhaps this situation was urgent enough for them to see the need for professional assistance.

Unfortunately, even though the parents gave indications that they would seek help, they did not follow through with continued counseling for Susan. She completed her elementary school career at our school, with continued referrals for anger related incidents. She began to receive assistance through a special education program at school which helped somewhat to manage the daily behaviors, but did nothing to get at the underlying issues related to her anger. She had very specific plans that we used to help her complete her fifth grade year.

Through it all Susan would have some good days where she would write notes to me or the counselor letting us know she was "being good." She desperately wanted to stay out of trouble and cognitively could recognize some of the issues she was dealing with. She simply was unable to recognize her triggers or respond appropriately when the anger got the best of her.

Susan is a young woman in her twenties now. I wonder how many times she has been handcuffed.

Lessons Learned

I learned that a child can be a real threat to others.

Even when the answer seems obvious, parents don't always agree.

Anger can be dangerous.

Acceptance

Jaron Dalton
Charlie Kelly
Dan Crankson
Robert Spursia
Ricky Langley

Jaron Dalton

" And the police came and there were guns in the closet, but the rat was under the chair, and my mommy got hurt, and the bad people went away."
Jaron, age seven

"Yes ma'am, there was a disturbance at the Dalton residence last night. No, we can't tell you who was involved. The children will be staying with the grandmother for awhile. No, there was no medication at the house for the boy."
Police Officer

There was a lot they didn't teach me in "principal school." I never dreamed I would work so closely with police officers, detectives, social workers, child abuse investigators, therapists, counselors, psychiatrists, and ministers. Jaron was a small third grade boy, developmentally delayed, but placed in a regular classroom. He struggled to sit in a chair, to pay attention, to comply with the simplest of requests. He had been diagnosed with attention deficit disorder and was taking Ritalin. He had a brand new principal and a brand new teacher that third grade year.

What he didn't have was a stable home life, the support of parents, or the many experiences that most children draw upon in school to make sense of what they are learning. A visit to his home to meet his mother introduced me to the rat under the chair – a real rat, but fortunately a dead rat. Jaron took great pleasure in showing me the rat as I tried to talk with his mother. His mother was very young and had issues of her own, involving heavy drug use. Because of my frequent visits to his home, my license plate was being run by the local police department to check for outstanding warrants. The drug traffic in the apartment complex where Jaron lived occurred day and night, and the local police had not yet determined that I was the new elementary school principal simply trying to reach out to a needy student.

Jaron's teacher, Sabrina, was beginning her teaching career and was one of the most talented first year teachers I had ever worked with. Jaron had captured her heart, as well as my own. We worked with the school nurse each day to make sure he got his required medication, but we suspected his mother was taking it herself or selling it. We developed special plans and lessons just for Jaron to help him learn. There were 28 other children in the class as well, so Sabrina was devoting long hours and much effort to her planning and preparation. Jaron's behaviors demanded a great deal of attention and time from both of us. After months of work, Sabrina came to me, close to tears, frustrated that she could not help Jaron and feeling like she was not giving her best to her other students because of all the time spent with Jaron.

I did quite a bit of soul searching after that conversation. As a principal, I was charged with doing what was best for all the students in the building. I realized that Jaron was not the only child needing special help and recognized the fact that I had gotten so personally involved with the needs of one child, I was not addressing the needs of others. After that revelation, Sabrina and I worked with other school personnel to help Jaron, and we spread the responsibilities for his learning among additional staff. Jaron moved away at the end of the third grade. I have often wondered what happened to him.

Lessons Learned

A balanced perspective is important.

Beginning teachers can teach principals.

We can't solve every child's problems, but we can love them in the midst of the turmoil.

We don't have to handle everything by ourselves.

Charlie Kelly

A chemistry textbook almost as big as he was, tucked under his arm, was Charlie's prize possession, ready for show and tell in his second grade classroom. To say Charlie was different from the other children in his class was an understatement. He was an incredibly bright child, with blonde hair, blue eyes, pale skin, and a delicate frame. He was personable and articulate, relating well to both children and adults. His mother was a nurse, and his father a scientist from an Eastern European country. Charlie was happy child, and almost on a daily basis provided some antic or statement that his teacher would readily share with me.

Charlie's physical education teacher stopped by the office before school started one day and casually mentioned that she had been meaning to tell me, but kept forgetting, that Charlie told her his dad had hit him hard with a board. After I got over the shock that she could forget something like that, I contacted the school nurse so that she could check on Charlie. Within minutes I got a call asking me to come to the clinic where sweet, beautiful Charlie lifted his shirt so I could see his back. His body was almost completely covered with bruises of all shapes, sizes, and colors. It was all I could do not to cry. When the social worker came to the school, she called for a police officer after seeing the bruises, and they took Charlie with them.

I remember sitting in my office, ready to sob, filled with sadness, grief, anger, helplessness, and yet I knew I had a teacher candidate sitting in the outer office waiting for an interview. I mentally changed gears, put on my happy face, walked to the door to greet the candidate with a pleasant smile, and conducted an interview. That was one of the hardest things I ever did.

When Charlie was in middle school, he killed himself.

Lessons Learned

Life can be very, very sad.

There are times we must play a role even when we don't feel like it.

Sometimes we are powerless to help, no matter how much we try.

The unexplainable happens.

Dan Crankson

Late in the school year, Mr. and Mrs. Crankson arrived for an appointment with me. They were considering enrolling their son Dan in our school. Dan was one of two children, both of whom had been adopted at birth. The Cranksons' children had attended private schools, so I was naturally curious as to why they were looking at their local public school as the school of choice midway through the elementary grades. In answer to my question about why they were making a change, they stated that Dan had been playing ball with some of the boys who attended our school and they thought he would enjoy being in school with these friends. When I asked if Dan had any special needs, the answer was an emphatic no. In fact, they stated that Dan was very bright and would need to be challenged academically.

When the Cranksons met with the school counselor the next day, more of the story came to light. Dan had been in four previous schools and had been asked to leave his current school because he hit a school employee. This incident occurred even though Dan had a one on one shadow monitoring his behavior, and was in a class of only ten children.

In the many meetings that followed, more of Dan's history was shared. The parents had been working with a pediatric neurologist, a psychiatrist, a psychologist, a counselor, a therapist, and had

72

tried a variety of treatments including a comprehensive workup related to nutrition, and vitamins and minerals. The parents were also receiving counseling to help them with their own parenting skills as they worked with Dan. His official diagnosis at that time was Oppositional Defiant Disorder. He had been asked to leave two schools and Dan had expressed his feelings about that by saying "I have failed twice," which the parents were very concerned about as they saw a boy who was beginning to have some significant self esteem issues. His father reported that Dan would pray at night "Please God, help me with my behavior." Dan's greatest fear was that he would not be able to hold it together.

Dan's parents described him by saying that on an intellectual level, Dan knows that his behavior needs to improve, and that after the fact, he can identify his poor choices and the undesirable consequences that follow. His difficulty is that in the middle of a situation, his emotions, his impulsivity, and his need for control seem to take over and he is unable to think rationally and make good choices. His parents reported that at the age of nine, Dan had been unable to be successful, regardless of how hard he tried. They observed Dan's frustration which led to negative talk about himself and to hitting himself by banging his head against a wall. In addition, he would use inappropriate language and destroy property. His own loss of control would scare and embarrass him.

The psychologist who evaluated Dan saw his ability to read social cues as similar to that of a much younger child. He indicated that Dan seemed disconnected emotionally and intellectually. Dan was described as a reactive child, unable to reflect on his own behavioral choices.

Dan came to our school in the fall to begin his third grade year. He was tall for his age, solidly built, a good athlete. Upon meeting him the first time, I was impressed by how articulate and personable he was. He smiled and appeared to be a genuinely delightful child who was excited to be coming to a new school.

On the third day of school, Dan became disruptive and defiant in the classroom, refusing to respond to his third grade teacher, nor his special education teacher who was called to intervene. He would not respond to me, his principal, and he threw stuffed animals, turned over chairs, and hit both his teacher and me while in my office. He was suspended from school. On the day he returned, I received two separate reports about incidents on the playground and also had a parent call complaining about Dan and his actions toward her child.

During Dan's third grade year, Dan had numerous serious discipline referrals including defiance, disrespect, inappropriate language and gestures, and verbally and physically assaulting students and staff members. He was on a very specific behavior plan and his parents consistently provided consequences at home. They included all the outside professionals in the support system that surrounded Dan so that he could learn from his bad choices and improve his behavior. His mother even spent time at school monitoring Dan's behavior during the lunch period since that was a particularly difficult time for him. He ended the year much as it began with a serious incident during which Dan cursed at students and staff, ran away, kicked and hit his teacher, and caused significant damage to the furnishings in the principal's office.

Dan's fourth grade year was an improvement, although there were still significant issues and concerns including Dan bringing a knife to school. He was not planning to harm anyone, and his parents' interpretation of the situation was that Dan simply wanted to show off to his peers. Given his unpredictable episodes of rage in the past and the zero tolerance policy regarding weapons, Dan was suspended for the required number of days for this incident. He lost privileges he had earned in the Level System his special education teacher had implemented for Dan.

Throughout Dan's two years at our school, my heart ached for him and his parents. Here was a child who could intellectually tell you everything he should do, and who would promise he would do better – and would be totally sincere in his desire to follow the rules and behave as he should. And then, when he was in the middle of an episode, he was unreachable. He would not listen and could not take control of his anger and his emotions. He did improve at times in this area, but not for substantially long periods of times.

Dan's improvements at our school came as a result of the intense efforts on the part of his parents, outside professionals, the school counselor, and three especially gifted teachers who loved Dan, who accepted him, and who held him accountable for his behavior. Those teachers spent untold hours in meetings, on phone calls, and in conferences working to find yet another approach to help this child. They spent sleepless nights worrying about him and what the future held for him.

Dan left our school to attend middle school in the same district. He lasted a few months there before he was sent to a military academy. I did see him on television, being interviewed at a political rally that his parents attended. Just watching him as he interacted with the reporter, I thought that no one watching would ever believe the other side of this personable young man.

The last time I saw Dan, he was standing next to his mother at a relative's funeral. His family member died in an accident at an early age, and Dan is the one who found the family member. As a young man, he was tall and handsome, but he was unable to show emotion that day, and simply stood in the receiving line, woodenly shaking hands and accepting condolences.

Lessons Learned

We will never know the reasons why some things happen.

Life is complicated and inexplicable.

Success can be measured in tiny little bits.

Our paths cross the paths of others for a reason – a reason that remains unknown sometimes.

Robert Spursia

I only knew Robert for thirty-eight days. In those thirty eight days, he consumed almost all of my time as a principal. His file folder at the end of those thirty eight days was almost two inches thick.

Robert's parents had divorced, so he entered our school in the spring of his second grade year. His mom had moved to be close to family and was single parenting her two small children, since the father lived in another state. On his first day at his new school, Robert was disruptive both in and out of the classroom, even when he was alone with an adult. He used inappropriate language, ran away, laughed extremely loudly, and visited my office the afternoon of his first day because of his behaviors.

We quickly learned from his mother that Robert had been having difficulties even in preschool with screaming, tantrums, and oppositional behaviors. His medical records which we later received indicated a diagnosis of treatment resistant attention deficit hyperactivity disorder and possible Tourette's syndrome. While he had received medication as an intervention, counseling and behavioral modification were not as consistent. His parents viewed his needs differently, so as a result, inconsistency was the norm.

Robert used inappropriate language, kicked or hit other students, ran away, and then began to make threats. He hit adults and touched them in inappropriate places. He wanted to break his teacher's legs and lock her out of the room. He said he dreamed about killing his sister.

One of his more alarming statements was when he started talking about killing black people. Robert stated "I'll be stronger, we'll have stronger weapons. We will get a spy plane, a fighter plane to bomb them. I have a better idea. We'll kill all the females so they can't have any more babies. Then we'll kill the children and the black men and boys." He then said he would get an atomic bomb to drop on the black people; that they were stupid and they were black because they were covered in poop. He then digressed into quite a conversation about poop saying that his dad made poop at his job and that when they talked on the phone, his dad would fart into the phone and ask Robert if he could smell it. The same day this conversation occurred, Robert walked to the office with a teacher and told her he was going to kill her too.

Robert's conversations and actions became more sexual in nature, grabbing the crotch and breasts of a female aide, and telling other children "I'll give you a nickel to tickle my pickle." We consulted with his physician who, when asked for ideas on how we could best help Robert, replied with "other than a bullwhip and a bentwood chair?" When we described the sexual acting out, the physician's comment was "horny little sucker."

We learned that the physician who was treating Robert was somewhat controversial in the treatment protocols he used, prescribing very large dosages of medications. As educators, and not medical professionals, we were somewhat frustrated by the medical interventions being used at the time, especially since we saw no improvement in Robert's behaviors.

We met numerous times with Robert's mother in an effort to meet his needs while at the same time protecting the other students and the learning environment. We discussed other placement options since a regular classroom setting, even with an aide assigned to Robert, was not working. The mother reported that Robert was also unsuccessful in the after school care program and in neighborhood interactions. The plan at the end of the school year was for Robert to attend a school in the fall that was designed for children with his type of needs and that the summer would be spent with the medical professionals to design a multifaceted approach to treat Robert and the family as well.

I never saw Robert or his family after the end of the school year. I have often wondered about him, his sister, his mother, his father, and even the physician who was so unorthodox in his conversations with the school staff. Robert would be a young man now. Did he manage to overcome the significant behavioral problems he was having even at the young age of seven? Did he die at an early age? Is he incarcerated? Did he go to college and manage to succeed in spite of the difficulties in his early years?

Lessons Learned

A child and his mind can be a mystery.

Family dynamics can play a huge part in a child's ability to function in the world around him.

A professional is not always professional.

Sometimes we can only do what we can do, and then we must realize the issue is bigger than what we are able to address.

Ricky Langley

Fortunately the chair was too heavy for eleven year old Ricky to lift. He tried with all his might to throw the office chair across the room, screaming "I'm really getting mad now." Prior to this outburst, Ricky had rolled his slight body into a ball with his head on his knees. He was crying and stating that he was the only one who gets blamed and that "everyone labels me." Ricky had been sent to my office for yet another discipline referral. He would become very agitated and extremely angry over seemingly small issues. Today's trip to the office was a result of his emotional outburst and disrespect to his teacher when he thought classmates had called him "beaver teeth."

After attempting to throw the chair, Ricky ran from the office and hid behind some shrubbery in the back of the school. After the counselor and I located him, she sat with him in the bushes talking quietly with Ricky, trying to help him become calm. This was not the first time Ricky had left the classroom or office. We had been working with his parents and grandparents for a number of years trying to get the psychological support Ricky obviously needed. Today Ricky told the counselor repeatedly that he wanted to kill himself and knew exactly how he would do it. He described using a knife and claimed that no one loved him and that he hated himself. He yelled "I just want it to end."

Ricky had been enrolled in our school since first grade. At that time his parents reported that he was working with a therapist on "adjustment problems." They indicated he had difficulty getting along with others. Throughout his time at our school, Ricky struggled behaviorally and emotionally. While the parents expressed great concern about Ricky and his needs, they seemed to remain in denial about the serious nature of Ricky's situation. Ricky received special education and individualized counseling at school. We also adjusted his school schedule and the length of the school day to help him be successful. While his parents did provide outside medical intervention for Ricky, they did not seem fully aware of the danger he could be to himself and others.

When Ricky told the counselor he wanted to end it all, he insisted she leave him outside alone in the cold. She told him he could come to her office and be alone there, but he refused, grabbed a broken piece of glass and threatened to cut her to pieces. The nurse and I then helped the counselor escort Ricky back into the office where we waited for his parents to arrive. The counselor who worked with Ricky outside the school setting worked at a local mental health facility. He was contacted and he encouraged the parents to bring Ricky in for an immediate evaluation. The parents did take Ricky to the mental health facility, but decided not to have him admitted. Neither did they follow up with a recommendation for Ricky to see a child psychiatrist or therapist.

After continued outbursts and situations that significantly disrupted his learning and that of the other students in his class, Ricky was placed in a self-contained class for students with significant behavioral and emotional concerns. The class was located in another school, so we did not hear much about Ricky until the end of the following year when his mother sent us a copy of a school award that indicated Ricky had not been in a fight for a whole month. Attached to the award was a note from his mom, which read "Spread the Good News – Ricky is and <u>always</u> has been a well behaved student."

While we were pleased to hear that Ricky was being successful in the very structured setting where he was now placed, we were concerned that his parents were still unable to see the severity of his needs. I have often wondered how the teen years were for Ricky and his family. He would be a young man now, and I wonder if he has been able to overcome his feelings of anger and paranoia that were obvious even as a very young child.

Lessons Learned

Time, energy, effort, and desire do not guarantee success.

We can communicate using all resources at our disposal, but the message is not always received.

You must consider the greater good when making decisions.

Parents love their children, but are not always capable of seeing how their love blinds them to the truth.

Perseverance

Susan McAdams
David Larson
David and Donald Turner
Caroline Abernathy
Wayne Hawkins

Susan McAdams

Susan was a chubby sixth grade girl who was best friends with Janelle. Together, they were a silly, giggly, chattering twosome, typical of prepubescent females. In my rational mind, I knew they were not conspiring against me. Neither were they plotting to make my life miserable, but on some days, it certainly seemed that was the case.

The girls were in my homeroom class and also came to me for math. The four sixth grade teachers taught in a departmental model and the students rotated through the four curricular areas – math, science, social studies, and language arts. We taught reading and spelling to our homeroom students. Neither girl was a scholar, but that was due more to the preoccupation with their social lives than any lack of cognitive ability.

In an effort to build relationships with Susan and Janelle, I invited them to our apartment on a Saturday to bake cookies. Their parents brought them over and we had a wonderful time together. I wish I could say that the time spent outside class had a powerful effect on their academic performance, but things continued pretty much as before. They were still very chatty in classes and were focused on all the things that occupy twelve year old girls, certainly not academic content.

The year was over before we knew it and the girls moved on to middle school. As is the case with teaching, my life was filled with the "new crop" of students entrusted to my care in the years that followed.

Years later – twelve to be exact – I ran into Susan and her mother at a local store. Susan was married and had a toddler with her. As we stood there talking, Susan suddenly said "there's something I need to tell you." I listened as she told me that in middle school and high school, she and Janelle had remained friends. During that period they were hanging out with others who were making bad choices. They were getting into trouble both at school and at home. Her parents were frantic and tried sending her to a counselor and to their pastor, but nothing seemed to impress Susan. Then she told me that I was the reason she stopped doing the things that were getting her into trouble and that she even broke off her friendship with Janelle. I can remember saying "How? I didn't even see you in high school." Susan then said that every time she was doing something she knew was wrong, a voice in her head would say "what would Mrs. Stanfield think of this?" That tiny voice is what nudged her into moving into a positive direction and was the reason she was happy and healthy now. Of course, I cried, her mother cried, and Susan cried. The toddler then began to cry because we were all crying! We parted ways that night and I kept Susan's words in my heart as an encouragement to draw on when a child seems unreachable. I treasure the gift Susan gave me.

Lessons Learned

We have great power to influence the lives of others.

We don't always know when we are making a positive difference for someone.

We may have to wait years to hear a thank you.

Never get discouraged – surprises come when you least expect them.

David Larson

Energy plus! David was one of those kids that put a smile on your face even when he was doing something he shouldn't be doing. He had the "gift of gab" as well and generally could talk himself out of any situation. For a nine year old third grader, he had the street smarts that made you think of a slick used car salesman, but he was just so doggoned cute!

Our school district participated in a desegregation program in which children who lived in the inner city could apply to attend schools in the suburbs. David was a "deseg kid" who came to our school with a sense of wonder and excitement. He quickly made friends and became a leader in his class. During his time at our school, he became friends with a number of the boys who lived in the area close to the school. He visited their homes and even stayed overnight at times.

David did not invite the local kids to his home however, because he and his mom lived with different family members and even spent time in a shelter for the homeless. You would never know that from David's demeanor though. He truly was one of the happiest kids I ever met. He was mischievous however and at times was on the receiving end of school consequences for his misbehavior. He handled that with his characteristic good humor, even calming down a group of his peers when they thought he had been unfairly punished. He quickly told them he did wrong, he admitted it, and there was no need to be so upset.

David loved his African American heritage and he prepared to deliver Dr. Martin Luther King's famous "I Have A Dream" speech at a school assembly. When he took the stage, he had an incredible presence. He walked with authority to the center of the stage and boomed forth those powerful words. The students were mesmerized; as they listened to a classmate bring history alive. The adults were awed and touched by David's performance, especially those who knew the particulars of his personal situation.

When I retired after quite a few years as an elementary principal, the parent organization held a reception on a Sunday afternoon. They had punch and refreshments and had planned a short program where they had planned to present the school with a gift in my honor. Most of those attending were families of children attending my school, but some former students had heard about the reception and dropped by to offer congratulations.

David not only dropped by, he asked to go on stage and deliver his own words of congratulations and thanks for the time he had spent with me. I cried.

David told me he had moved in with one of the local families, and had attended a local high school. He was in the process of deciding where he would attend college.

Lessons Learned

Dreams do come true.

Where you come from does not determine where you will go.

Teenage boys can be caring and compassionate.

David and Donald Turner

The Turners had seven children, five boys and two girls. Four of the five boys were diagnosed with cystic fibrosis, neurofibromatosis, and diabetes. I met the Turner family at a summer camp for children with disabilities or serious illnesses. The first year, only the four oldest children attended camp and they were miserably homesick. The two oldest, Dick and Emily, managed to adjust pretty quickly. Dick had some medical issues but he was in relatively good health. The two youngest, David and Donald, cried and refused to eat. Their cystic fibrosis was aggravated by the hot weather so they spent a lot of time in the air conditioned clinic. I was a volunteer and worked wherever I was needed and that summer I spent many hours with David and Donald. I think I was a mother figure for them, and I helped ease the homesickness a bit. By the end of the week, both boys were enjoying some of the activities and were reveling in all the special attention they were receiving from the college counselors.

The boys lived in a neighboring town so I saw them a few times after summer camp. David was the older of the two and his cystic fibrosis was more severe. He spent a great deal of time in and out of the hospital and would usually call me when he was admitted. I met the younger children in the family, including Danny who had a large tumor on the side of his face, which affected both his speech and his vision. It did not affect his smile, however! He was one of the happiest children I had ever met, so glad to see you and talk with you. He never got frustrated when people had a hard time understanding him. He would simply keep repeating the words with gestures and motions until his meaning was clear. The youngest of the seven was Drew, and he appeared to be healthy. The other girl, Emma, was a beautiful child, quiet and shy.

The children attended camp for a number of years so our connection became stronger. I spent many holidays visiting David, Donald, and Danny in the hospital. There were times that all three boys were hospitalized at the same time. Danny had surgery for the tumor, but the damage to his vision, speech, and also his hearing was irreversible. His bright eyes would just shine above the scar that ran from his ear by his nose, and down to his mouth. Donald seemed to respond to the treatments at the hospital, and even though he had to be hospitalized frequently, he was able to recover enough to go home. David had more difficulties and his prognosis was not good. David's breathing got much worse and he was unable to eat and digest his food. David died at the tender age of twelve.

The funeral for David is the first one I attended for a child and my heart broke for his parents and his brothers and his sisters. Mr. Turner was a hard working father who worked a factory job to support his family. Mrs. Turner was a quiet, soft-spoken woman, who deferred to her husband. When

I visited the boys in the hospital, it was almost always Mr. Turner who was there with them. With seven children, and all the medical concerns, the Turners had learned to accept help from agencies and organizations, although they were very proud and wanted to be self sufficient. At David's funeral, Donald was the one who was greeting people who had come to offer their condolences, including many of the doctors and nurses who had worked with the family since the children were babies. As an eight year old, he was remarkably mature, thanking people for coming, and maintaining a strong outer appearance. I wondered if he realized that the disease that had killed his brother was what he was battling. I wondered if he thought about his own death at a young age. As I drove home that evening, I could remember David's face as he splashed in the pool at camp and how happy he was to be "a normal kid" that one week at camp. I was thankful he was no longer suffering.

I recently received a phone call from Dick Turner, the oldest of the children, and as soon as I heard his voice, I was afraid that he was calling to tell me that Donald had died. The last time I had seen Donald, he was really struggling with all aspects of his disease, and was unable to attend school. Dick, however, was calling to tell me that their father had passed away, suddenly from a heart attack.

I attended yet another funeral for this family and was struck by how devastated all of them were. Mrs. Turner never once stepped away from the open casket, and did not respond in any way to the greetings or hugs of those who were there. Dick was trying to be the man of the family but was having a hard time holding back his tears. The oldest girl, Emily, was worried about her mother who had not eaten or slept since their father had died. The three youngest, Danny, Emma, and Drew, seemed oblivious to what was happening. And poor Donald was so fragile and weakened from his illness, he simply sat and stared. As I sat with him, together with some of the former camp counselors, we tried to offer him support and comfort. This fourteen year old, who looked about the size of a ten year old, just looked at us, and said "we will be okay. We know how to deal with all this. Don't worry about us." Two years later, Donald died at the age of sixteen.

Lessons Learned

Children are stronger than we are at times.

Perseverance in the midst of struggle is a gift.

Life's challenges make us stronger.

Caroline Abernathy

Late one evening about 6pm......I was sitting in my office catching up on the paperwork and waiting to attend the parent teacher executive board meeting; the outer office lights were dimmed and the door locked; a sharp rap was heard on the door; I looked up and saw a woman in a suit, beckoning to me.

That was the night I met Caroline's mother. She was a lawyer and had stopped by our school on her way home from work. She told me that she had heard good things about our school and how we worked with disabled children. Her daughter had cerebral palsy and other needs including impaired vision and she wanted her to attend our school. Since school boundaries in the district were determined by where a child lived, I asked Mrs. Abernathy for her address. They did not live in our attendance area. I explained the attendance policy and she left, but assured me she would be back, and that her daughter Caroline would be starting school with us in the fall.

Months later, after letters were sent and pleas were made to the district offices, Caroline did indeed enroll in our school. She used a walker but had very little stamina and strength to walk long distances. Our building was all on one floor and was quite large. The physical education classes were held at one end of the building and other special classes like art, and music, as well as the library and computer class were in the opposite end of the building. The distances from the classrooms to special classes, the playground, the nurse's office, and the cafeteria were long.

At the end of Caroline's first year with us, she was able to walk all over the building with her peers. At an evening event near the end of school, her parents were so pleased because she basically "ran" from one end of the school to the other three times showing her parents all her special projects in each class and then ending the night doing the "duck dance" with all of the other children and parents.

Caroline's vision was such that the vision specialist recommended the use of Braille so that Caroline could learn to read. Because of her physical limitations, writing was not even an expectation. By the end of third grade, Caroline, who still had difficulty seeing more than a few words on a page, was reading enlarged materials with over one hundred words on a page. She was using the computer to compose sentences and could dictate answers to questions for homework or tests. She also worked very hard to be able to write with a pencil and was able to write her name and about ten different words on paper. Instead of taking spelling tests with only five words and missing half of them, Caroline was able to study fifteen words and only miss one or two each week.

Her parents sent a letter to all the school personnel who had worked with Caroline describing her remarkable academic and physical progress. The parents were amazed and pleased given the earlier prognosis given to them by Caroline's physicians. Caroline was very motivated by her peers and would try hard to meet the same expectations. She developed independence and self confidence by participating in all aspects of the school day. In her PE classes, she loved both gymnastics and modern dance and her parents reported that she was able to do a trunk rotation in gymnastics that far surpassed anything they had been able to accomplish in her private physical therapy. Because of the dance unit, Caroline wanted to walk barefoot, and was able to keep her heel flat for the first time despite the spasticity in her legs.

Her parents wrote that Caroline had become so much more independent, wanting to bathe and dress herself, and she was willing to try almost anything. She made friends easily and was invited to visit the homes of other children. She was truly "included" in a regular education setting and flourished. Her parents provided a great deal of support and outside therapy and activities. Her teachers held high expectations and yet provided the support she needed to meet those expectations. And her peers motivated her to be like them, by simply being themselves. Caroline's academic, physical, and social progress during the five years she attended school with us was amazing. What amazed me most was this beautiful child's determination and will to succeed.

When Caroline had first arrived at school, people noticed her thick, long hair, her smile, and the difficult way her body twisted and moved when she tried to push her walker. They had difficulty understanding her speech. When Caroline left, she still used a walker, but was able to walk much more smoothly, holding her head upright. She was easily understood and that smile of hers could light up the building. Her self confidence and independence were an inspiration to her classmates and to the adults who had the privilege of working with her.

I recently opened a newspaper and saw beautiful Caroline in the photo accompanying a story about high school students invited to Washington, D.C. as part of a local social studies program. Older, yes; independent, yes; self sufficient, yes…. and with the same smile from years ago, a real testament to her achievements and her hard work to succeed in a non-disabled world.

Lessons Learned

Even the significantly disabled can succeed.

Our own concerns should not place limits on a child's potential.

High expectations must come with support and encouragement.

Peer pressure can be a positive motivator.

Wayne Hawkins

How can such a tiny child evoke such a strong reaction from adults? Wayne Hawkins crashed into our world when he arrived for kindergarten and quickly made it known that he did not want to be there. Wayne was the youngest of three children in a family that defined "dysfunctional."

Our first substantial contact with the family was an emergency meeting called when Wayne's older brother, William, left the school grounds without permission, describing the voices in his head that told him to go to the local gas station. In reality, the consensus was that William had gotten angry when asked by his second grade teacher about some incomplete work and had deliberately waited behind his class as they entered the building from recess. He simply kept walking, and even though the teacher noticed his absence almost immediately, he had made his way to the gas station to call his mom and report that he was hearing voices.

The children lived with their mother Janae, but the father also came to the meeting. William Sr. was quiet but threatening in his body language. When he crossed his legs, the ankle bracelet he was wearing was visible. It was obvious that there was tension between the parents and the meeting was uncomfortable for all who were there. While the focus of the meeting was concern for William and his recent behaviors, it quickly expanded into a concern for the general well being for all of the children in the home.

After the father left, Janae shared her frustrations at being the single parent responsible for the day to day needs of supporting her three children, with a father who appeared sporadically and then wanted to make the decisions. William Sr. was on house arrest and had known drug problems. He did not help financially, but intimidated Janae. A restraining order was being ignored and she was afraid to report him to the police. She worked two jobs and as a result, left Wayne, age 5, William, age 7, and Winona, age 9 at home alone most evenings. The children were told never to answer the door or go outside when their mother was at work. They reported many fights and arguments among the three of them when they were at home without adult supervision.

Classroom teachers, the school counselor, the nurse, and I worked with Janae the entire time her children attended our school. One day she surprised us totally when she appeared in the school office with two older children and said she wanted to register them for school. Apparently the older children were Janae's as well, but they had been living with a friend. Their addition to the home was not a smooth process. The older children – a boy and a girl – bullied the younger three and threatened them if they reported anything to the school or to Janae.

The entire home situation helped to explain Wayne's behaviors. He was one of the most stubborn children I have ever met – obstinate did not even begin to describe him. His very patient, compassionate, loving kindergarten teacher was brought to tears on more than one occasion when she was unable to persuade Wayne to do the simplest of tasks – many times tasks that were pleasant, such as picking up his snack from the snack table and moving to another table to eat.

All of the school personnel who worked with Wayne's family devoted many hours to helping the family and providing outside resources to assist Janae and the children. Winona was quiet and withdrawn at school, but ruled her younger brothers with a vicious mouth and a heavy fist at home. Eventually, William's behaviors at school escalated to the point where he needed a more restrictive classroom setting. The two older children created such havoc in the home that Janae sent them back to live with her friend, a situation we never quite understood. William Sr. would show up unexpectedly at school and threaten his children if they misbehaved. His inconsistent attempts at providing parental input simply caused additional problems with the children and with Janae.

Wayne's stubborn responses to almost any request continued throughout his kindergarten year. First grade did not bring much improvement. I remember clearly a sunny fall afternoon about ten minutes before dismissal. Wayne refused to pack up his book bag to go home and then removed his shoes. Nothing his teacher said or did could convince him to prepare for the bus ride home. She finally had a teacher assistant escort him to the office when he began to scream and disrupt the classroom, frightening the other children.

Wayne arrived in my office and my attempts at humor to diffuse the situation were unsuccessful. Wayne hopped onto the credenza in my office, swinging his legs and making bumping noises against the wood. He glared at me and the swinging became more pronounced. As a last resort, I decided to try reverse psychology on this six year old and told him that whatever he did, I did not want him to put on his shoes and ride the bus home. I then walked out of my office and stood in the outer office for a few minutes. When I returned, there he sat, off the credenza and in a chair, shoes on, book bag in his lap, with a huge grin on his face. I responded with what I was actually thinking " Wayne, you are a piece of work." And I will never forget his response…….. " And you are a piece of trash!"

Needless to say, I was thrilled when he marched out and boarded the bus in time for his ride home. A part of me was truly dreading sitting with this young child for the better part of an afternoon waiting for his mom to get off work and come to school to get him. I could only imagine what life was like at home since Wayne was struggling so mightily to have some control over any aspect of his life.

I ached for Janae as a young mother trying to do what was best for her children but limited by her own fears and the need to meet basic survival needs. We continued to support the family through additional crisis situations and turmoil. I was awed by Janae's willingness to keep trying, even when most people in her situation would have simply given up. Many times, she was so tired she was barely able to talk. And yet, throughout the years we worked together, she was always willing to do what was asked of her to help her children.

Lessons Learned

Perseverance and persistence are admirable and essential qualities for both parents and teachers.

We cannot give up, no matter how difficult the situation.

A child's actions can be a cry for help – we must listen.

Advocacy

Brian Mann
Kaitlin Carson
Billy Frampton
DeWayne Puckett
Clark Warner

Brian Mann

I had heard about the Mann family for years, but this year was my first year to have one of the Mann children in my class. I confess that even as an experienced sixth grade teacher, I was a bit concerned about teaching one of these children. The family was a large one – eleven children and a baby on the way. The father was not involved in school affairs and there was not much discussion about him. I do remember hearing that the parents locked food in the trunk of the car so that the children would not eat without permission. Of greater concern was the common knowledge that the mother was a grand genie in the local Ku Klux Klan, a vocal racist, and an assertive and aggressive woman.

Brian was a small, slightly built boy, quiet, and a loner. The other children had heard stories from the neighborhood and many had been directed to stay away from the Mann children. Brian was a bed wetter, and on many days, smelled of stale urine. That situation did not endear him to his classmates. I found my heart touched by this gentle child, who, through no fault of his own, had been born into a less than desirable family situation. He struggled with his learning, but willingly worked with me one on one when we could find the extra minutes. I delighted in the times that I was able to get a smile from him. Sadness was an ever present reality for Brian.

As the year progressed, it became obvious to me that Brian was simply not ready to go on to the middle school. His academic performance was weak, his maturity level was that of a much younger child, and physically, he was smaller than most of his peers. I approached my principal, seeking permission to recommend retention, something that was seldom done, especially with a sixth grade boy. He gave his reluctant permission based on the evidence I had presented to him, with the stipulation that I be the one to talk with Brian's mother about the possibility. If Mrs. Mann was opposed to retention, I was not to pursue it further.

I had talked with Mrs. Mann throughout the school year, so the concerns were not new for her. I was more than a bit nervous when she arrived for the conference where I had planned to recommend retention. She listened, she glared, she did not speak. I carefully presented my case, expressing my concern for Brian, and my desire for him to be successful. She then looked at me and said," I will agree to this on one condition." I had no idea what her condition might be and was afraid it would be something the school could not honor. She then stated very emphatically that the only way Brian would be in sixth grade again was if he could be in my classroom again. I almost fainted, but assured her that we could arrange that.

Brian spent two years with me. The second year he was somewhat of an assistant because he knew the routines and expectations and he quickly became my helper. He took great delight in knowing the surprises I had in store for the class as we covered the academic content and celebrated special events. I lost contact with Brian shortly after he moved on to middle school and high school, but I never forgot him. He touched my life in a powerful way.

Lessons Learned

Children don't choose their parents.

Parents care about their children and want what is best for them, even if the parents appear very different from the norm.

The quiet loner needs attention as much, or more, than the demanding child.

Be willing to fight battles that benefit children.

Kaitlin Carson

She stood in the bathroom screaming, pouring the pine scented cleanser on the floor, smearing it with her hands over every inch of the dirty tile floor. The slippery pink soap pooled in an obscene shape on the floor of the clinic.

"Get Dr. Stanfield here," the counselor commanded. Barb, the school secretary made the calls.

"What's your approach to discipline?" The question hung in the air late on an October afternoon. The middle aged woman cleared her throat for the sixteenth time and began to stumble through her answer. I tried desperately to focus on her response and appear truly interested but mentally I had already crossed her off the list of potential substitutes for our school district. Even though it was my birthday, I had said yes when the call had coming earlier in the day begging for help with the annual substitute teacher hiring fair. More applicants had arrived at the middle school library than expected. In a weak moment, I had agreed to leave my school a half hour before dismissal to help with interviews.

I had talked with quite a few good applicants, but the current interviewee was clearly not cut out for the challenges of substitute teaching. The secretary of the middle school appeared in the library, whispered to the coordinator of the substitute fair, and looked in my direction. I immediately wondered what was wrong. Being a school principal does that to you. You are hyper sensitive to sounds, actions, looks, and silences. I knew before she walked over to me that the birthday plans I had for the evening would not materialize.

"Your school called and you have an emergency. They need you." I grabbed my purse, made a quick apology to the would be sub and headed to my car. When I arrived at school, I went straight to the office. Barb saw me coming and said only two words – "it's Kaitlin."

I could hear her screams piercing the normally quiet office. The clinic adjoined the office and even though the door was closed, there was no mistaking the sounds emanating from the nurse's office. When I entered the clinic, I saw Joan, the school nurse, breathing hard, and smelling of pine. The school counselor, Sue, looked at me with eyes full of concern. Sue was about fifty years old and had been the counselor at our school ever since I had been there. We had been through a lot together and I trusted Sue without question. Her compassion for kids and their families kept her at school late into the evenings. She was a jewel and I depended on her insights and experience with children.

"It's Kaitlin – she's flipped out again. There is no talking to her or calming her. She ran out of her classroom when her teacher asked her to get her things out of her cubby and get ready to go home. When I got to her, she was trying to run and leave the building, so I held her and managed to get her here. We have tried to calm her, but she has been just like she was the last time. We have called her mom and she refuses to come get her – said to call the ambulance again and she will have the doctor meet them at the hospital."

There was no sign of Kaitlin and in response to the puzzled look that must have been on my face, Joan quickly pointed to the bathroom door. That is when I saw the soap on the floor and noticed for the first time that both Sue and Joan had damp areas on their clothing. The scent of pine was extremely strong and I was still trying to make sense of the closed door, the smells, the mess, and the screams. Sue, reading my mind as she frequently did, quickly informed me that Kaitlin had run into the bathroom and locked the door when they had gotten her to the clinic. She had emptied the soap dispenser and smeared pink soap all over the floor before pouring the pine scented cleanser onto the tile floor. Both Sue and Joan were covered with soap and cleanser from their efforts to unlock the door and from trying to restrain Kaitlin as she kicked, screamed, and tried to bite them.

Kaitlin was a beautiful child, with skin the color of chocolate. On good days, her eyes sparkled like topaz jewels and she smiled with such sweetness that even the hardest of hearts would melt. She wore her hair in braids with beads or barrettes on each meticulously braided strand. On days like today though, her hair was an unsightly mess with stray hairs sticking out all over her head, no semblance of braids. Her eyes were glazed and I could smell the anger and fear when I slowly looked into the clinic bathroom. Kaitlin stood in the corner wedged between the toilet and the ceramic wall, glaring in such a way that I knew she did not even see me.

I could hear the paramedics' arrival in the background and wondered if Kaitlin heard them. The last time they came for her, she walked out on her own and climbed into the back of the ambulance as if she did it regularly – with no fear or apprehension about going to a hospital with people she did not know. Joan and Sue were briefing the men on the situation, giving them all the necessary information about Kaitlin and her history.

"Kaitlin, it's Dr. Stanfield," I said gently, as I eased my way into the tiny bathroom. My shoes slid on the slick floor and the pine scent overwhelmed me. "We have talked to your mom and she wants you to see the doctor like you did before. Mom is going to meet you at the hospital and they are going to help you." Without a word, she lifted her arms up, almost as if she were a toddler begging to be picked up. I reached for her hand to walk her out and her body went limp.

"Kaitlin, do you want to walk or do you want me to carry you?" Again, she lifted her arms. I was surprised by her response because whenever we had episodes like this in the past, Kaitlin absolutely refused to allow anyone to touch her. There had

been times she had been so out of control in my
office that she had thrown any item close to her, had
screamed and yelled, and stuck her fingers in her
ears. Out of desperation, I had simply lucked into a
strategy that helped calm her when I put a blanket
on the floor near her. She covered herself with it,
peeking out to see if I were watching, and then
slowly quieting until she fell asleep. When she
awoke, she had been almost catatonic, and walked
as if her legs were weighted. It was only after what I
later referred to as "sleep therapy" that I was able to
get Kaitlin to respond to my requests. Given that
there had been no "sleep therapy" today, I was
puzzled by her willingness to let me touch her.

I lifted her and carried her as I would an
infant or toddler, with her head on my shoulder. She
was completely relaxed and her body was dead
weight. For a six year old, she was tall and her legs
were long. The paramedics followed us out the
main door and down the steps to the bus lane where
the ambulance was parked. By this time the local
fire department and police department had also
dispatched officers, so we had quite an assortment
of emergency vehicles in front of the school.
Fortunately, dismissal had occurred about thirty
minutes earlier so there were no other students or
parents there to see Kaitlin as she left. She allowed
me to place her on the gurney and she lay as still as
death on the white surface, not making a sound. It
was eerie – not at all the response I would expect
from a six year old child on her way to the hospital.

Kaitlin attended our school for five years before her psychiatric needs required placement in a school that provided therapy as a part of the program. As a toddler, Kaitlin had witnessed the murder of her father. Her mother was a young woman trying to do the best she could, but she was overwhelmed by Kaitlin's emotional needs, her own stress due to the fact she had to miss work so often for Kaitlin, and the lack of mental health treatment easily available to low income families. The bureaucracy associated with health care for those with minimal insurance was a huge mountain of discouragement, and it was only after a local psychiatrist decided to take Kaitlin's case without cost, that the family began to receive any assistance. At the school level, we provided support as much as possible, but without professional medical and psychiatric support, our efforts were unsuccessful.

I would visit Kaitlin, even after she and her mother moved away. The last time I saw Kaitlin, she was thirteen and was planning to be back in a regular classroom in a regular school. She had been diagnosed with a mental illness but was being treated medically and appeared to be able to function in the regular world of school. Her mother had a new baby and Kaitlin was excited about being the big sister.

I remember reading some of Kaitlin's journal entries that she would share when I visited her during her hospital stays. She was an excellent writer, a smart girl, and I still think about her and what she may be writing in her journal now.

Lessons Learned

Caring is not enough.

Persistent, aggressive efforts are needed at times to help children.

A child's early experiences can have a significant impact on a child

A child can have a profound impact on the adults in her life.

Billy Frampton

*"Remember that tomorrow is the special pizza
lunch for the fourth graders – don't forget to bring
your permission slips for the trip to the park.
Congratulations to Sam Kelly for his first place
finish in the community track event. We are proud
of you, Sam. And now, let's have a great day here at
Garrett School; do your best! Oh, I almost forgot,
we are thrilled to announce that allergy season
ended yesterday!"*
*.......... morning announcements over the public
address system*

Billy Frampton arrived at Garrett School
like a tornado whipping through Kansas. He was a
small child with dark eyes and dark hair, but his
energy and constant motion more than compensated
for his small stature. As a five year old
kindergartener, he was placed in an all day program
with nineteen other five year olds. His parents, both
professionals, were filled with not only the normal
apprehension that comes with sending their "baby"
to big school, but also with great concern and real
fear about how Billy would respond to being in a
"normal" setting with "normal" kids. Billy had been
diagnosed with Asperger's and his parents had
spent many, many hours and a great deal of effort
making sure Billy had all the resources and support
he needed to be successful.

Billy was obviously a smart youngster who learned the academic skills fairly easily. Where he struggled was with social skills. He was easily frustrated by the simplest of expectations, he refused to go to the bathroom without adult assistance, he was a perfectionist who would cry and scream if he made a mistake, and he would perseverate over the strangest things. He had a difficult time relating to the other children who tried to be friends with him.

His kindergarten teacher was a marvel. Even though there was minimal information available regarding working with children who have autistic tendencies, she studied on her own and worked closely with Billy's parents to address each individual issue or concern. She sought assistance from the special educators, the counselor, the nurse, and the principal whenever she was stymied by a particular behavior or response. Thus the morning announcement shared above – Billy had decided he was allergic - we were never sure what he thought he was allergic to – but he would not stop blowing and rubbing his nose. It had gotten so sore and red that scabs were beginning to form. All of our earlier efforts had failed and the adults in the building were concerned and frustrated that we had not been able to extinguish that particular behavior. Totally out of desperation and without planning, I simply decided to announce that allergy season was over. The rest of the students and teachers in the school were puzzled by my announcement, but those who worked with Billy knew exactly why the announcement was made. And, hallelujah, it worked! Billy heard that important announcement over the intercom in his room and immediately stopped the blowing, rubbing, and picking. His teacher later told me that Billy seemed to think that the voice over the intercom was God's voice

Billy added great joy to life at Garrett School – he was so happy to be there everyday, and he gradually began to improve his social skills, with much dedicated work from many people who reinforced on a daily basis his behavior when he did what was expected. He learned that he could not tear up his paper every time he made a small mistake. He learned that he could cross out a mistake instead of erasing so hard he made holes in his paper. He learned how to share with his classmates. One of my treasures is a picture of Billy and a little girl in his class, both dressed in the frilly satin dress up clothes with tiaras on their heads. Billy loved the feel of the satin and was quite content to dress up even when many of the boys were busy playing with the blocks.

We all celebrated the day Billy learned to care for his own needs while in the bathroom. I confess we did laugh when his teacher reported how she taught him to wipe himself from outside the bathroom door. "Billy, you use the tissue and then look at it. If it is still brown, you throw the tissue away and get more and do it again. Keep doing that until the tissue isn't brown anymore." Where was that instructional strategy taught in the teacher preparation program?

Billy's mother knew what a challenge Billy was in a typical classroom setting. She regularly called, emailed, and wrote expressing her thanks and appreciation for everyone's efforts. She was constantly seeking the newest research and information that could benefit Billy and she shared that with all of us. She truly was a partner in Billy's education. Billy was not the smartest child in the class, neither was he the child with the greatest challenges. Billy was sometimes truly in his own world, but we could honestly say that while at Garrett, Billy was learning and he was happy.

Lessons Learned

Parents are valuable partners.

Joy is contagious.

We don't really know what "normal" is.

Celebrate each small step of success.

Creative solutions to frustrating problems can come without warning or planning.

DeWayne Puckett

Mrs. Puckett had three children, Shaniqua
Bryson, DeWayne Puckett, and DeWon Puckett. All
three children had been affected by lead poisoning
from the lead embedded paint in the apartments
they had lived in as toddlers. Mrs. Puckett worked
three different jobs to provide for her children, and
yet, she would take time from work and ride the bus
to school anytime she was needed for meetings or
conferences about any of her three children. Mr.
Puckett was not as involved with the daily
happenings but would respond when called for help
with his children. Shaniqua was well behaved most
of the time, but struggled to learn. She was
persistent and just would not give up. DeWon, the
youngest, was a fun loving youngster, who was
about as wide as he was tall. He too, did his best
most of the time, even though school was hard for
him. DeWayne was another story.

DeWayne was a fourth grade student who
was referred to the office on a regular basis for
fighting, kicking, hitting, stealing, lying, and for
disrespect and defiance of the adults who worked
with him. DeWayne's behaviors had been an on-
going concern and his mother had worked with a
physician and a counselor to address the problems.
She was adamant about making sure he got the
services he needed so that he could "amount to
something." At times, Mrs. Puckett was
confrontational, offending some of those who were

present at the meetings because she asked probing questions and demanded answers with great detail. She did not make excuses for DeWayne, but she did not want him accused of misbehavior without evidence to support the concerns.

We tried all sorts of interventions with DeWayne, with a special behavioral plan for him that involved the counselor and a special education teacher. His mother shared how much he liked keeping up with sports statistics, so that was used to motivate him to complete his work and follow the school rules. What I found interesting about DeWayne was that his facial expressions could be sullen and angry one minute, and then devoid of all expression the next. He also was a master at passive aggression. I remember one day having him walk with me from the office to the room where we had in school suspension. I don't think I have ever seen a child walk so slowly, knowing full well that he was irritating the life out of me! He could engage any adult in a power struggle, just by sitting silently and refusing to respond in any way when asked a question or asked to complete a task.

As maddening as his behavior was for us at school, his mother expressed similar frustrations with him at home. He antagonized his siblings and refused to do what was asked of him at home. Mrs. Puckett was worried about DeWayne and what his future would be, given his attitudes and behaviors at the young age of ten. The counselor insisted that the father be more involved in DeWayne's life and asked that the school contact him when DeWayne misbehaved at school. We did that, but ultimately it was Mrs. Puckett who would follow through.

DeWayne was eventually moved to a class for children with similar needs and did not attend our school the next year. I remember walking the hall with him, my pace a fast clip, and his slower than a snail. What I remember most was the unconditional love Mrs. Puckett had for her child, even when she was extremely frustrated by his actions. She was not a professional with a lot of education, but she knew her child and she refused to give up on him, no matter what it took – daily notes and calls, meetings, doctor visits, medication, counseling, assignment notebooks, a structured behavior plan for school and home. She stands out in my memory as a real advocate for her child, and not a parent who would say "don't call me. I am at work and I deal with him at home. When he is at school, he is your problem." Mrs. Puckett loved her son, and as difficult as it was for her to deal with all the problems, she never gave up trying to help him.

Lessons Learned

Every child needs an advocate.

A parent's love and devotion to a child can be challenged on a regular basis.

Confrontational parents are good for us – they hold us accountable.

Clark Warner

I had no administrative experience and had decided that I must have lived my entire life inside a protective bubble. My college classes in administration did not address some of the situations I was called upon to handle. I did not have experience with some of the horrific life circumstances that young children endure. I can remember that first year as a principal thinking two thoughts frequently – they didn't teach me this in "principal school" and I want all children to live in "country nice."

Clark was a small, delicately featured, blonde second grader, seven years in age, much older in life experiences. He was a quiet child, not disruptive at all. In fact, he was somewhat withdrawn, but not so much that he stood out in the classroom as someone with problems. Little did we know.

Clark went to the nurse with a stomachache one day and in the course of talking with her, revealed in a very matter of fact voice that he was tired of living and that he planned to kill himself with a sharp knife that he slept with each night. Clark was a new student in our school, so we did not know much about the family. As he talked to the nurse, he shared more details about what was going on at home, including the fact that the government was hiding them and he wasn't supposed to tell anyone. He was scared of his stepfather and reported that he would hide when his stepfather got mad at his mom, because that is when he would hit them. He said his mom cried a lot because the stepfather made her dance in a club late at night way across the river.

Much later we learned that the stepfather was in the witness protection program and was scheduled to testify in a major drug case. He was not really married to Clark's mother but they had lived together for about five years. She was an exotic dancer at a club in a neighboring state. On the day Clark talked to the nurse, I called his mother and asked her to come to school. I spent time talking with Kate, Clark's mother, and she hesitantly told me how frightened she was living with Dwayne, but she had nowhere to go and could not support herself and Clark. She would glance nervously at the door the entire time we talked, afraid Dwayne would show up.

I explained how the local Division of Family Services could provide help and support for the family and that given the severity of the situation, we were required to make a call to report concerns about Clark's safety and well being. We did not want to create more hardship for her, but wanted to get her some help so that she could leave the situation if she wanted to do that.

By late that afternoon, the nurse, the counselor, Kate and Dwayne, a case manager from social services, a police officer, and I were meeting in a small conference room trying to help the family and be sure that Clark was safe. Dwayne was a huge man, with arms and a chest that bulged under his shirt. He was very verbal, hardly allowing anyone else to speak. Even though he did not make any overt threats, there was an underlying threat in almost everything he said. He was not happy that the school was involved with his family, and angry that social services had been called. The more he spoke, the more I knew that Clark needed to be out of the home for his own safety and well being.

The hours passed and the nurse and counselor both had to leave. I stayed with the parents and the social worker as we continued to try to resolve the concerns. The police officer had been called by the social worker to be present, but he was more an observer than participant. At one point, I stepped out of the room with the social worker, and pleaded with her to remove Clark from the home at least temporarily. She said the police officer had to be the one to make that decision. I was still so naïve about the workings of this agency, I did not know who else to call, or where to seek additional help.

I remember driving home that night about nine o'clock after everyone simply went their separate ways, crying as I drove, thinking that this could be the night Clark kills himself....or gets beaten to death for telling us about his family. I insisted that the police officer take my home phone number so he could call me if anything happened during the night.

A few days after that long, long meeting, Clark did not come to school. When we called home, the number had been disconnected. Students who lived in the same area reported that one day they were living in their apartment and the next day they were gone. The police would not tell us anything about the family and where they had gone.

To this day, I can see Clark's face and I wonder if he ever escaped the fear and the sadness that was his life at the tender age of seven.

Lessons Learned

Sometimes we care so much it hurts.

Our own ignorance can prevent us from being effective.

When you don't know how to help, don't give up.

Be assertive and persistent when you know it is what is best for a child.

Lessons Learned
My Reflections

Lessons Learned

As I searched my brain for the memories I have shared about these children, I would stop at times and simply let the memories wash over me. Tears would flow and my heart would ache. Other days brought smiles and sweet thoughts.

Throughout the entire reflective process, I have felt immense gratitude for each of the lessons learned as a result of knowing and loving these precious children and their families.

Advocacy

I do not deceive myself – I realize that our world is not a beautiful place for many children and their families. I know that as principals, counselors, and teachers we cannot change every child's situation, but I do know, without a doubt, that each of us can make a positive difference in the lives of the children whom we serve. We may be the one to plant an idea in a child's mind, an idea that much later develops fully because of the actions of other people. We must be advocates for children, and for entire families, especially when their voices are weakened through the difficult life circumstances that challenge them daily. We have all experienced situations where decisions are made for a child because the parents are informed, vocal, and insistent, and where a similar situation – with a different child, whose parents are hesitant and uninformed – could result in the opposite decision. Our moral obligation to our children requires that such a disparity in results does not occur. I am reminded of Dewey's quote "What the best and wisest parent wants for his child, that must the society want for all its children." We must act as the best and wisest parents for the children entrusted in our care.

Humility

While it is great to assume that we indeed have the wisdom of the best and wisest parent, we in fact are human beings who share common failings. We don't always have the right answers. We don't always make the best decisions. We allow personal feelings to interfere with objective thinking. We make mistakes and we have a hard time admitting those errors in judgment. We become defensive when someone questions our decisions. The most freeing lesson I learned as a young teacher was not to take criticism personally. When I was able to begin looking at a situation objectively, truly with a problem solving mindset, I was freed from the emotional complications that accompanied difficult situations. When I reminded myself that in the large majority of cases, that everyone concerned really had the best interests of the child in mind, I was able to listen more carefully, hear more clearly, and respond more thoughtfully. Being willing to admit mistakes and take responsibility for a poor decision helped me to make connections with the others involved. Most people simply want an acknowledgement of errors in judgment, and then they are willing to accept and move forward.

Respect

For people to work together and move toward a common goal, even in difficult and emotionally charged situations, there must be mutual respect. Respect does not happen automatically. Respect comes from many experiences over time, interactions where we prove ourselves as honest, caring, ethical people who can be trusted.

As educators, we work with people who may be very different from us, who may have different values and lifestyles, who may not be as educated, who may come from different backgrounds or cultures. I have found, that regardless of the differences, we share many similarities. We want children to have the best possible experiences in the school and community settings. We want to protect children from harmful, hurtful influences. We all want to be heard and understood. We want to be valued and accepted. We want to be treated with respect.

The building of relationships is a critical piece of mutual respect. As a teacher, and later as a building principal, I would make personal phone calls and send handwritten notes as often as possible, in an effort to connect with the parents and families with whom I worked. I worked hard at being available when someone was angry, upset, or hurting, so that a personal contact was made when emotions were high.

Building relationships takes time and the sad truth is that in our schools today, we are inundated with demands for our time – meetings, reports, test scores and data analysis. A mantra I repeated often helped me keep the focus on the students, the teachers, and the families – "People are more important than paper." You can analyze data at home at midnight, but you cannot comfort or listen to a student, teacher, or parent who needs you. Connecting with others on a personal level is the foundation upon which mutual respect is built.

Acceptance and Perseverance

Probably one of the hardest lessons I learned as an educator, and one that I can continue to struggle with, is that despite all our desire, our time, our energy, our prayers, and our hard work, that sometimes we are going to lose. We will not be able to make a positive difference in someone's life. We will not be able to address all the issues that need to be addressed. We will be met with hostility and anger by the very ones we are seeking to help. There will be times that the unthinkable happens – a child dies, a family is devastated by financial ruin and medical emergencies, a former student makes horrible choices and faces a life in prison because of those choices.

What I have learned is that there are times you simply have to realize that a particular battle is no longer yours to fight. In order to preserve your own sanity and the energy needed to help others, there are times you must accept that your influence is limited, that it is time to allow others with more resources, or a different approach, to step in and work with the child or family you are unable to reach.

With that being said, I have also learned that you don't step aside at the first sign of resistance or a problem. You persevere. You don't give up. You continue to make phone calls, home visits, and send personal notes. You look for the small steps toward success even when they are tiny. You seek support and additional resources and you take each day as a personal challenge to reach that child or that family that desperately needs support and encouragement.

I have found in most cases that the time to step aside becomes obvious when the situation becomes more clearly defined. When you have exhausted all avenues of support and resources to address a situation, and the solution requires medical, psychiatric, or legal intervention, you have to acknowledge that it is time to "pass the baton" to the next runner in the race. Your role has ended, at least for the immediate future.

Hope

Our schools must be havens of hope for our children. Our children must feel safe and know that they are loved and respected. They must know that they will be held accountable for their actions and decisions. They must know that there are caring, compassionate adults who love them enough to challenge them to meet high expectations. They must know that those same adults will provide support and encouragement every step of the way on the journey to meet those high expectations. We must give students a vision of what the future can be for them – especially for the children whose vision of the future is a limited and discouraging one.

The hope we have for the future must be evident. We must model for our children a positive approach to challenges, so they see us tackle difficult goals and accomplish them through cooperation, perseverance, hard work, and great effort. They need to see us handle disappointment and life's hard hits in a way that demonstrates that hard times are temporary, that possibilities still exist, and that success and happiness in life is possible.

Made in the USA
Monee, IL
05 May 2021

67827235R00085